This Text Book is useful for Sir Parashurambhau College of Arts, Science and Commerce, Pune. (Autonomous)

# Economics (S-3)

# International Economics - I

## T.Y. B. A. (Sem. - V) (Course Code : EC3517)

**Dr. Sudhir Suresh Dhore**
Asst. Professor
(MA, SET, M.Phil, Ph.D. Economics)
Shikshana Prasaraka Mandali's Sir Parashurambhau College, Pune.

2023

Price : 100/-

SUCCESS PUBLICATIONS

***Published by***
***Dr. Rajesh M. Patne***
**Success Publications**
Radha Krishna Apartment, 535, Shaniwar Peth,
Appa Balwant Chowk, Opp. Prabhat Talkies, Pune - 411 030.
Ph. 24434662. Mobile: 9325315464.

***Copyrights***
With the Publisher

***Printed at***
**Success Publications**
S.No. 30/27, Laxmi Industrial Estate,
Near Prabhat News Paper, Dhayari, Pune-41.

***Edition***
2023

***Edited By***
Mr. Valmik Gaikwad

***Typesetting, Layout***
Mr. Valmik Gaikwad

***Cover Designing***
Miss. Varsha Lokhande

# Preface

*It is a matter of great pleasure for us to present this book to our esteemed readers. This book has been designed as standard text on 'International Economics – I' for T.Y.B.A. (Sem. - V).*

*This book comprehensively covers the entire syllabus of T.Y.B.A. (Sem. - V) Course of Sir Parashurambhau College (Autonomous), Pune effective from 2021 onwards. It has been written to meet the requirements of students of T.Y.B.A. (Sem. - V) Some of the special features of the book are as follows:*

1. *Full coverage of the revised syllabus of T.Y.B.A. (Sem. - V).*
2. *Chapter outline at the beginning of each chapter to give a bird's eye view of the topics covered in the chapter.*
3. *Point wise explanation of each topic in the chapter.*
4. *Topics are logically arranged in numbered paragraphs exactly according to the modified syllabus.*
5. *Proposed questions at the end of each chapter.*
6. *Extensive use of diagrams, tables and various forms to give visual view of key concepts and techniques.*
7. *Conversational, lucid and simple language.*

*Every effort has been made to provide the readers with most up-to-date and authentic material on the subject.*

*We are very grateful to our publisher Mrs. and Mr. Rajesh Patne who have rendered all possible assistance in bringing out this book. We wish to acknowledge our deep gratitude to staff who have assisted and helped us in preparing this book. We will consider our efforts amply rewarded in case the book proves useful to the students and teachers of the subject.*

*Suggestions of readers are welcome and shall be acknowledged with gratitude.*

***With best wishes.***

***By Authors***

# Syllabus

**T. Y. B.A. (Sem. - V)**

**Economics S-3 (International Economics - I) (Course Code – EC3517)**

| Unit No. | Topic | Period |
|---|---|---|
| 1 | **Introduction**<br>• International Economics- Meaning, Scope<br>• Inter-regional and International Trade<br>• Importance of International Economics | 12 |
| 2 | **Theories of International Trade**<br>• Theory of Absolute Cost Advantage<br>• Theory of Comparative Cost Advantage<br>• Heckscher-Ohlin Theorem<br>• Leontief's Paradox<br>• Rybczynski Theorem<br>• Intra-Industry Trade | 12 |
| 3 | **Gains from Trade**<br>• Static and Dynamic Gains<br>• Terms of trade – Importance, types and determinants<br>• Reciprocal Demand and Derivation of Offer Curves<br>• Reasons for Unfavorable Terms of trade | 12 |
| 4 | **Balance of Payments**<br>• Balance of trade and Balance of payments<br>• Concepts and Components<br>• Equilibrium and Disequilibrium in Balance of Payments; Causes and Consequences<br>• Measures to correct deficit in the balance of p ayments | 12 |

# INDEX

**T. Y. B.A. (Sem. - V)**

**Economics S-3 (International Economics - I) (Course Code – EC3517)**

# Introduction to International Economics

UNIT 1

1.1 International Economics

1.2 Inter-regional Trade and International Trade

1.3 Importance of International Trade

## Introduction:

Today each nation state is an acknowledged and dominant political unit. Whole world is divided into different nation states. The foundries of these states may be changing but their existence is perpetual. Even though these states are different from each other, they are closely linked with each other. International economics is an independent branch of economics. It includes the study of trade between these states and the economical relations of these states, the independence of these states and their co-operation etc. With the revolutionary changes in means of transport and communication and with annihilation of distance, economic links among nations of the world are growing more and more, intimate with the consequence that any major economic change in any part of the world has almost immediate economic impact on the rest of the world. The subject of international economics is applied economics where many policy problems of empirical nature are elucidated and examined with the help of economic theories.

## 1.1. International Economics :

Today's world, no nation exists in economic isolation. All aspects of a nation's economy, its industries, service sectors, levels of income and employment, living standard are linked to the economics of its trading partners. This linkage takes the form of international movements of goods and services, labour, business enterprise, investment funds and technology. Indeed, national economic policies cannot be formulated without evaluating their probable impacts on the economies of other countries. International economics is concerned with the effects upon economic activity of international differences in productive resources and consumer preferences and the international institutions that affect them.

### 1.1.1 Meaning :

A branch of economics that deals with international relations, trade and forces that influence the domestic economy is called as international economics. It is gaining more and more importance day-by-day because of globalisation. International economics is mainly concerned with the study of economic relations between sovereign nations focussing on the international aspects of economic activities. International economics is concerned with the problems of consumption, production, exchange and distribution of the national product. International economics uses the same fundamental methods of analysis as other branches of economics because the motives and behaviour of individuals are the same in international trade as they are in domestic transactions.

### 1.1.2 Definitions :

Following are the definitions of international economics:

1) **Paul Krugman and Maurice Obstfeld:**

   *"International economics is the study of how economic interactions between countries shape the global economy. It examines the flows of goods, services, and capital across borders, as well as the policies and institutions that govern these interactions."*

2) **Robert C. Feenstra and Alan M. Taylor:**

   *"International economics is concerned with the economic interactions between countries, including the determinants of international trade and investment, the effects of trade policies, the causes and consequences of global economic imbalances, and the role of exchange rates and international financial markets."*

3) **Dominick Salvatore:**

   *"International economics is the branch of economics that deals with the economic relations among nations. It analyzes the determinants and consequences of international trade, the international movement of capital, and the international flow of technology and labor."*

4) **Paul R. Krugman:**

   *"International economics is concerned with the economic interactions between countries, focusing on the effects of international trade, international financial flows, and international economic policies on national economies."*

5) **Maurice D. Levi:**

   *"International economics is the study of economic activities that transcend national borders, including the determinants of trade and capital flows, the impact of globalization on economies, and the analysis of international economic policies and institutions."*

### 1.1.3 Scope of International Economics :

A branch of economics that deals with international relations, trade and forces that influence the domestic economy is called as international economics. It is gaining more and more importance day-by-day because of globalisation. Scope refers to the subject matter of international economics. It is divided into five categories. Scope of international economics is as follows:

1) **Theories of Trade :**
The theories related to trade try to find out the reasons "Why do the nation's trade". The classical economist, Sir David Ricardo, developed the theory of comparative cost. The Swedish economist Hecksher developed the Factor Endowment Theory. Modern economists have not developed a separate theory as they think that international trade is the extension of domestic trade. These theories help us in understanding the factors leading to international trade such as differences in costs and availability of factors of production.

2) **International Trade Policy:**
All countries give lot of importance to foreign trade. So they have their own policies regarding trade. International economics studies different trade policies such as free trade policy, protected trade policy etc.

3) **Foreign Exchange Market :**
Foreign market deals with the demand, supply and the price of foreign exchange and its influence on other macro-economic variables.

4) **Balance of Payments :**
Balance of payment gives an idea about external position of a country. Government can adopt suitable measures if there is disequilibrium in the balance of payments.

5) **International Trade:**
International trade is a central component of International Economics. It involves the exchange of goods and services across national borders. The study of international trade seeks to understand the determinants and patterns of trade, the gains from trade, and the impact of trade on various aspects of the economy. Key topics within international trade include comparative advantage, trade barriers (such as tariffs and quotas), trade agreements, trade liberalization, trade balances, and the role of multinational corporations.

6) **International Finance:**
International finance focuses on the flow of capital across borders, including foreign direct investment (FDI), portfolio investment, and international lending. It examines exchange rates, international financial markets, capital mobility, balance of payments, financial crises, capital controls, and the effects of global capital flows on national economies. International finance also studies the role of international financial institutions such as the IMF and the World Bank.

**7) Globalization:**

Globalization refers to the increasing interconnectedness and integration of economies and societies around the world. It is a multidimensional concept that encompasses economic, social, political, and cultural aspects. Within the scope of International Economics, the study of globalization examines the drivers and consequences of global economic integration, the impact of technological advancements on globalization, the role of multinational corporations in global production networks, and the effects of globalization on income inequality, labor markets, and economic development.

**8) Economic Development:**

International Economics also addresses the economic development of nations, particularly in developing countries. It explores the factors that contribute to economic growth, poverty reduction, and improvements in living standards. This includes the analysis of foreign aid, foreign direct investment (FDI), technology transfer, trade policies, and the role of international institutions in promoting economic development. Additionally, the study of economic development within International Economics often delves into issues related to income distribution, human capital, sustainable development, and poverty alleviation.

**9) International Economic Policy:**

The field of International Economics has significant policy implications. Governments and policymakers rely on the insights and analysis provided by International Economics to formulate and evaluate their economic policies in an international context. This includes policies related to trade, exchange rates, capital flows, investment, intellectual property rights, labor mobility, and regional economic integration. The study of international economic policy involves assessing the impacts and effectiveness of various policy measures, understanding the implications of policy coordination or conflict between nations, and analyzing the role of international institutions in shaping economic policy at a global level.

**10) Regional Integration:**

Regional integration refers to the process by which countries within a specific region come together to form closer economic cooperation and integration. This includes the formation of regional trade agreements, economic unions, and common markets. The scope of International Economics covers the analysis of regional integration initiatives such as the European Union (EU), North American Free Trade Agreement (NAFTA), and Association of Southeast Asian Nations (ASEAN). It examines the motivations, benefits, and challenges associated with regional integration, as well as the impact on participating countries and non-member nations.

**11) International Economic Institutions:**

International Economics also encompasses the study of international economic institutions and organizations that play a significant role in shaping global economic relations. These institutions include the World Trade Organization (WTO), International Monetary Fund (IMF), World Bank, and regional development banks. The scope of International Economics includes examining the roles, functions, and effectiveness of these institutions in promoting international trade, economic stability, financial assistance, and global economic governance.

**12) Trade and Environment:**

The interaction between international trade and environmental concerns is another important area within International Economics. It investigates the environmental consequences of trade, such as pollution, resource depletion, and carbon emissions. The study of trade and environment also examines the role of international agreements and regulations in addressing environmental issues, the potential conflicts between trade liberalization and environmental protection, and the concept of sustainable development.

### 1.1.4 Importance of International Economics :

Importance of International Economics can be explained with the following points:

**1) Understanding Global Interdependence:**

International Economics helps us comprehend the interdependence of economies around the world. It highlights how economic events in one country can have far-reaching consequences for other countries. This understanding is crucial for policymakers, businesses, and individuals to navigate the complexities of the global economy effectively.

**2) Facilitating International Trade:**

International trade plays a vital role in economic growth and development. By studying International Economics, we gain insights into the determinants and patterns of trade, the benefits of specialization and comparative advantage, and the impact of trade policies and barriers. This knowledge helps countries enhance their competitiveness, expand markets, and achieve mutually beneficial trade relationships.

**3) Promoting Economic Growth and Development:**

International Economics provides valuable insights into the factors that drive economic growth and development. It helps identify the role of international trade, foreign direct investment (FDI), technology transfer, and financial flows in fostering economic progress. Understanding these dynamics enables policymakers to formulate effective strategies and policies to promote sustainable development.

**4) Managing Global Financial Systems:**

International finance is a critical aspect of International Economics. It involves the study of exchange rates, capital flows, financial markets, and international financial institutions. Effective management of global financial systems is crucial for maintaining economic stability, managing currency fluctuations, and addressing financial crises. International Economics equips policymakers with the necessary tools to make informed decisions in these areas.

5) **Fostering Global Cooperation:**
International Economics facilitates global cooperation by providing a framework for addressing economic challenges collectively. Through international institutions such as the World Trade Organization (WTO) and the International Monetary Fund (IMF), countries can engage in negotiations, resolve trade disputes, and coordinate policies. These platforms are essential for promoting fairness, reducing trade barriers, and ensuring a stable and prosperous global economy.

6) **Addressing Income Inequality:**
International Economics helps address income inequality both within and among countries. By studying the distributional effects of international trade, investment, and globalization, policymakers can design policies that promote inclusive growth and reduce poverty. This includes measures to enhance access to education, healthcare, and social protection, as well as initiatives to promote fair trade and responsible investment practices.

7) **Anticipating and Managing Economic Risks:**
International Economics provides tools and frameworks for analyzing and managing economic risks on a global scale. It enables the identification of vulnerabilities, such as imbalances in trade, finance, or exchange rates, and helps in devising strategies to mitigate these risks. By understanding the interconnectedness of economies, policymakers can better respond to financial crises, market fluctuations, and other economic shocks.

8) **Supporting Business Decision-Making:**
Businesses operating in the global marketplace rely on International Economics to make informed decisions. Understanding international trade dynamics, exchange rate movements, and global market trends is essential for businesses to identify opportunities, assess risks, and develop effective international business strategies. International Economics provides the necessary analytical tools to navigate the complexities of the global business environment.

## 1.2. Inter-regional and International Trade :

Inter-regional trade is domestic or internal trade. On the other hand, international trade is a trade between two nations or countries. A controversy is going on among the economists whether there is any difference between inter-regional trade and international trade. According to classical economists, there is a fundamental difference between inter-regional and international trade. So, they put forward a separate theory of international trade which is known as theory of comparative costs. But modern economists like Bertil Ohlin contend that there is no intrinsic difference between inter-regional and international trade. The difference is of degree rather than of kind. Details of international trade do not differ in kind but they present problems regarding money and banking, wages and prices which are absent in inter-regional trade.

### 1.2.1 Inter-Regional Trade (Domestic Trade) :

It refers to the trade which is carried out in different places and regions of the same country. It is also called inter-regional trade. Trade between Haryana and Punjab or Uttaranchal and Bihar is an example of inter-regional trade.

**A) Meaning:**

Inter-regional trade refers to the exchange of goods, services, and resources between different regions or areas, whether within a country or across national borders. It encompasses the movement of goods, capital, and labor across regional boundaries and fosters economic integration, specialization, and cooperation. Inter-regional trade plays a crucial role in promoting economic growth, reducing regional disparities, and creating opportunities for regions to access markets, resources, and investment. It facilitates the transfer of technology, knowledge, and skills, contributing to innovation and regional development. Overall, inter-regional trade is a fundamental driver of economic activity and regional interconnectedness.

**B) Characteristics of Inter-Regional Trade:**

Inter-regional trade exhibits several distinct characteristics that differentiate it from other forms of trade. Here are some key characteristics of inter-regional trade:

**1) Geographic Scope:**

Inter-regional trade involves economic transactions and exchanges that occur between different geographic regions or areas, whether within a country or across national borders. It refers to trade flows between distinct regional entities, such as states, provinces, or countries.

**2) Regional Specialization:**

Inter-regional trade often arises from regional specialization, where different regions focus on producing goods and services in which they have a comparative advantage. Each region utilizes its specific resources, skills, and factors of production to specialize in particular industries, creating opportunities for mutually beneficial trade.

**3) Comparative Advantage:**

Inter-regional trade is driven by the principle of comparative advantage. Regions engage in trade to benefit from the differences in their resource endowments, technology, and production capabilities. By specializing in the production of goods and services that they can produce most efficiently, regions can maximize their productivity and overall economic welfare.

4) **Transportation and Infrastructure:**
The physical movement of goods and resources is a critical aspect of inter-regional trade. Efficient transportation systems, logistics networks, and infrastructure play a significant role in facilitating the smooth flow of goods between regions. Adequate infrastructure, including roads, railways, ports, and communication networks, is essential for reducing transportation costs and enhancing inter-regional trade.

5) **Economic Linkages:**
Inter-regional trade fosters economic linkages and interdependencies between regions. It creates economic relationships and networks of suppliers, buyers, and service providers, strengthening regional cooperation and integration. These linkages contribute to the transfer of technology, knowledge, and skills, promoting innovation and regional economic development.

6) **Regional Economic Integration:**
Inter-regional trade often serves as a catalyst for regional economic integration. It can lead to the formation of economic blocs, free trade agreements, or regional trading arrangements, where regions come together to deepen economic ties, eliminate trade barriers, and foster greater economic cooperation. Regional economic integration aims to enhance trade flows, promote investment, and create a more integrated and seamless regional market.

7) **Policy Implications:**
Inter-regional trade has policy implications for governments and policymakers. It requires the formulation of trade policies, regional development strategies, and infrastructure investment plans to support and promote inter-regional trade flows. Policies related to tariff and non-tariff barriers, investment incentives, transportation infrastructure, and regional cooperation frameworks all have an impact on inter-regional trade dynamics.

8) **Regional Disparities:**
Inter-regional trade can contribute to reducing regional disparities by providing opportunities for less-developed regions to access larger markets, attract investment, and participate in value chains. It can help stimulate economic growth and development in regions with comparative advantages in specific industries, contributing to regional convergence.

### 1.2.2 International Trade :

International trade is a trade between two or more than two countries. Trade between India and U.K. is called international or foreign trade. The goods consigned from India to U.K. will be known as India's exports. On the other hand, goods coming from U.K. to India will be called India's imports. International trade is a central component of International Economics.

**A) Meaning:**

International trade is the exchange of capital, goods, and services across international borders or territories. In most countries, such trade represents a significant share of gross domestic product (GDP). While international trade has been present throughout much of history, it's economic, social, and political importance has been on the rise in recent centuries. Industrialisation, advanced transportation, globalization, multinational corporations, and outsourcing are all having a major impact on the international trade system. Increasing international trade is crucial to the continuance of globalisation.

**B) Definitions :**

Definitions of International Trade are as under:

**1) Wasserman and Haltman :**

*"International Trade consists of transactions between residents of different countries."*

**2) Ellsworth :**

*"International Trade is simply the extension of the trade beyond the boundaries of a nation."*

**3) Edgeworth :**

"*International Trade means in plain English trade between nations.*"

**C) Salient Features of International Trade :**

The following are the distinguishing features of international trade:

**1) Immobility factor :**

The degree of immobility of factors like labour and capital is generally greater between countries than within a country. Immigration laws, citizenship, qualifications etc. often restrict the international mobility of labour. International capital flows are prohibited or severely limited by different governments. Consequently, the economic significance of such immobility of factors tends to equality within but not between countries. For instance, wages may be equal in Mumbai and Pune but not in Mumbai and London. According to Harrod, it, thus, follows that domestic trade consists largely of exchange of goods between producers who enjoy similar standards of life whereas international trade consists of exchange of goods between producers enjoying widely differing standards. Evidently, the principles which determine the course and nature of internal and international trade are bound to be different in some respects at least. In this context, it may be pointed out that the price of a commodity in the country where it is produced tends to equal its cost of production. The reason is that if in an industry, the price is higher than its cost, resources will flow into it from other industries, output will increase and the price will fall until it is equal to the cost of production. Conversely, resources will flow out of the industry output will decline; the price will go up and ultimately equal its cost of production. But, as among different countries, resources are comparatively immobile; hence, there is no automatic influence equalising price and costs. Therefore, there may be permanent difference between the cost of production of a commodity in one country and the price obtained in a different country for it. For instance, the price of tea in India must, in the long run, be equal to its cost of production in India. But in the U.K., the price of Indian tea may be permanently higher than its cost of production in India. In this way, international trade differs from home trade.

2) **Heterogeneous Markets :**
   In the international economy, world markets lack homogeneity on account of differences in climate, language, preferences, habit, customs, weights and measures etc. The behaviour of international buyers in each case would, therefore, be different.

3) **Different National Groups :**
   International trade takes place between differently cohered groups. The socio-economic environment differs greatly among different nations.

4) **Different Political Units :**
   International trade is a phenomenon which occurs among different political units.

5) **Different National Politics and Government Interventions :**
   Economic and political policies differ from one country to another. Policies pertaining to trade, commerce, export and import, taxation etc., also differ widely among countries though they are more or less uniform within the country. Tariff policy import quota system, subsidies and other controls adopted by governments interfere with the course of normal trade between one country and another.

6) **Different Currencies :**
   Another notable feature of international trade is that it involves the use of different types of currencies. So each country has its own policy in regard to exchange rates and foreign exchange.

## 1.2.3 Similarities and Differences between Inter-regional and International Trade:

A comparison between (domestic) trade and international trade can be made by analysing the similarities and differences between the two. Generally, domestic trade takes place within a country from state to state, or place to place to meet the needs of the people. In other words, differences in demand and supply cost and prices among states of different places give rise to exchanges of goods and services domestically. This can be a cause of international trade also. But there are certain other determinants that differentiate internal and international trade.

**A) Similarities between Domestic and International Trade:**

Similarities between Domestic and International Trade Domestic trade and International trade bear the following similarities:

1) **Specialisation:**

The basis of domestic and international trade is specialisation which is the result of division of labour. If a state or region in a country specialises in the production of a given commodity, then the other states or regions of that country buy that commodity from that state instead of producing the same themselves. For instance, Maharashtra and Gujarat states have specialized themselves in the production of cotton textiles and U.P. in the production of sugar. These states meet the demand for cloth and sugar of all other states. Likewise when different countries specialise in the production of different goods then the same are exported to other countries. For example, Bangladesh has specialised herself in the production of jute manufactures and United States in the production of machines. Consequently, United States exports machines and Bangladesh exports jute manufactures to rest of the world.

2) **Cost:**

Both domestics and international trades aim at producing goods at low cost. Goods are sent out of that region in a country where the same are produced at a low cost to other regions. For example, cost of production of rice and fish is comparatively less in Andhra Pradesh. Thus, Andhra Pradesh should produce rice and fish and send to other parts of the country. Similarly, in international trade goods are imported from that country where the same are produced at low cost. In this way, both" internal and international trade provide maximum satisfaction at low price.

3) **Exchange:**

The aim of both kinds of trade is mutual exchange of a variety of goods. Exchange aims at procuring those goods which are either not available at all or are available in a very small quantity at a particular place in exchange for its surplus production. It can, therefore, be said that exchange is the goal of domestic and international trade.

4) **Profit:**

The aim of the producer, whether in domestic or international trade, is to earn profit Under domestic trade, a producer would like to sell his goods at that place where he can get maximum profit Similarly, under International trade the producer of a country would like to export his goods to those countries where he is likely to get maximum profit

5) **Mutual Co-operation:**

Traders under internal trade, move from one state to the other. It leads to close trade relations and a spirit of co-operation among them. Under international trade also economic relations encourage mutual cooperation in social and political spheres as well.

6) **Voluntary Transactions:**

Transactions in both kind of trade depend on the discretion of the people. Government of a country may restrict, or even prohibit, trade with another country, but it cannot force the people into buying and selling of a particular good.

**7) Consumer's Sovereignty:**

Be it domestic trade or be it international trade, producers produce those goods which are liked by the consumers.

**B) Difference between International Trade and Domestic Trade:**

There are several reasons to believe the classical view that International Trade is fundamentally different from Inter-Regional Trade is as follows:

| Points of Comparison | International Trade | Domestic Trade |
|---|---|---|
| **Use of Currencies** | Different currencies of different countries are used in international trade. e.g. Rupee, Dollar, Yen, Pound, etc. | Only one currency is used in internal trade. E.g. In India Rupee is the currency for used domestic trade. |
| **Meaning** | The trade between two or more countries beyond the political and geographical boundaries is international trade. | The trade within the political and geographical boundaries is internal trade or domestic trade. |
| **Factor Immobility** | Labour and capital are regarded as immobile between countries. Labour is not mobile because of differences in languages, customs, occupational skills, unwillingness to leave familiar surroundings and family ties; high travelling expenses to foreign country and restrictions imposed by the foreign country. The immobility of capital is due to political uncertainty, ignorance of prospectus of investment in foreign country, imperfections of banking system and instability of foreign currency. | They are perfectly mobile within a country. There is a complete adjustment to wage differences and factor price disparities within a country with quick and easy movement of labour and other factors. Such problems do not arise in the case of inter-regional trade. |
| **Different Markets** | International markets are separated by differences in languages, usage, habits, taste, etc. | National markets are often separated from rest of the international markets by their peculiar individualities such as metric and non-metric units of measurements, different and |

| | | |
|---|---|---|
| | | peculiar tastes, traditions, habitual preferences of certain type of commodities. |
| **Problems of Balance of Payment** | Problems do not arise in the case of international trade. | There is greater mobility of capital within regions than between countries. When the value of imports exceeds the value of exports, the balance of payments is in disequilibrium. The policies adopted by the country to correct disequilibrium in balance of payments such as devaluation, exchange control, import restrictions or export promotions will give rise to a number of other problems. |
| **Transport Costs** | Trade between countries involves high transport costs. | The transport costs are low in internal trade. |
| **Different National Policies** | International trade, there are artificial barriers in the form of quotas, import duties, tariffs, exchange control, etc. on the movement of goods and services from one country to another. | Policies relating to commerce, trade, taxation, etc. are the same within the country. |
| **Different Political Groups** | In international trade, there is no cohesion among nations and every country trades with other countries in its own interests | Inter-regional trade or domestic trade is among people belonging to the same country even though they differ on the basis of castes, creeds, religions, tastes or customs. They have a sense of belonging to one nation and their loyalty to the region is secondary. |
| **Degree of Competition** | Much more competition | Lesser competition since it is restricted to internal firm. |
| **Demand and Supply** | Demand and supply cannot work out their full effects where foreign trade is concerned. | Such factors can work out their full efforts in the case of internal trade. |

| | | |
|---|---|---|
| **Import and Export Restrictions** | No restrictions are ordinarily imposed on the sale purchase of goods in different parts of the country but in the interest of national development and security, government of different countries do impose some restrictions on the import and export of some goods. | In order to discourage import and export of some other goods, tariffs are raised substantially. On the contrary, no such restrictions or tariffs are imposed in use of internal trade. These restrictions call for a separate theory of international trade. |

## 1.3. Importance of International Trade:

There are some advantages of international trade described as follows:

1) **Full use of Natural Resources :**
   International trade enables the natural resources to be exploited fully. Under-developed countries are not in a position to use their own mineral resources. Such countries export their raw materials to developed industrial countries where the same are needed the most.
2) **Cheap Goods :**
   Because of international trade, all countries get goods at cheap prices. It is so because every country produces those goods in the production of which it has to incur less comparative cost.
3) **Power to face Natural Calamities :**
   When natural calamities like famine, flood, epidemic etc. befall a country then other countries come to its rescue. Thus, all countries are enabled to face these calamities squarely.
4) **Varieties of Goods :**
   By virtue of international trade, consumers get an opportunity to consume large variety of goods produced by different countries. This way, aggregate consumption of all countries increases leading to higher standard of living of their people.
5) **Surplus Production :**
   International trade enables every country to dispose of its surplus production. Some countries produce more goods than their own requirements. This surplus production sells in other countries and, thus, avoid fall in their prices within the country. Consequently, the country exporting goods earns foreign exchange that leads to its economic prosperity.
6) **Competition :**
   International trade encourages countries to vie with each other in the production of different kinds of goods at low cost of production.

**7) Wide Market :**

International trade widens the extent of the market. Every country makes an attempt to produce different goods in large quantity and thereby enjoys internal and external economies. Law of increasing returns operate into export industries. It lowers the cost of production.

**8) End of Monopolistic :**

There are more opportunities of producing goods when the same are to be exported among different countries. New entrepreneurs enter the industry and monopolistic tendencies come to an end.

**9) Availability of Raw Material :**

Some countries of the world are in possession of advanced technical know-how but they lack raw material. Such countries are enabled to import raw material from road through international trade and thereby attain industrial advancement of their economy. For distance Japan has very little quantity of iron-one within its national boundaries yet it has reached the highest stage of industrial advancement by importing iron-ore from other countries.

**10) Specialisation :**

On account of international trade, different countries specialise in the production of those goods alone in which they enjoy favourable production conditions. As a result, goods produced in large quantity at low price and in line quality.

**11) Possibility of Economic Development :**

International trade enhances the possibility of economic development of different countries. By importing machinery, technical know-how and other ancillary equipment from developed countries, underdeveloped countries make the optimum use of their available natural resources and raw material. They are, thus, enabled to increase their output and exports and thereby promote economic development. In the words of Robertson, "International trade is an engine growth."

**12) Improvement in Techniques of Production :**

International trade stimulates the spirit of competition among the entrepreneurs. Novel techniques of production are devised to produce quality goods at low cost. Advancement of technology is the key to economic development.

**13) Advantage to Different Classes :**

Advantages of international trade are not confined to a particular class rather all classes; producers, consumers, labourer's etc. stand to thereby.

**14) Increase in National Income :**

International trade helps in the advancement of all spheres of production. More capital is invested in export industries. It has a dual effect on the economy as more people are employed and more exports take place. On account of both these developments, investment and foreign trade multiplier come into operation resulting in a manifold increase in national income.

**15) More Employment :**

All sectors of the economy viz. agriculture, industry, transport, banking, trade etc. develop as a result of international trade and thereby generate employment opportunities.

❖❖❖❖❖❖❖❖

## Review Questions

**Q. 1. Answer in 100 Words:**

1) Explain the Scope of International Economics.
2) State the Features of Inter-regional Trade.
3) Explain the Characteristics of International Trade.

**Q. 2. Answer in 200 Words:**

1) Explain in detail Meaning and Scope of International Economics.
2) Discuss the Importance of International Economics.
3) Explain the differences between Inter-regional and International Trade.

**Q. 3. Answer in 400 Words:**

1) What is International Economics? Explain the Scope and Importance of International Economics.
2) Discuss in detail about the Inter-regional Trade.
3) What is International Trade? Explain the Importance of International Trade.
4) Explain the Similarities between Inter-regional and International Trade.

**Q. 4. Write Short Notes on:**

1) Concept of International Economics.
2) Inter-regional Trade.
3) International Trade.
4) Similarities between Inter-regional and International Trade.
5) Differences between Inter-regional and International Trade.

❖❖❖❖❖❖❖❖

# Theories of International Trade

# UNIT 2



## Introduction:

It has grown enormously in modern times. Today, on a global average, nearly 15 percent of the national product ends up in foreign markets and an almost equivalent percentage of the domestic consumption is met by goods imported. In the case of developing countries, this ratio is about 20 percent. A very pertinent question in this context, therefore, is why do nations engage in trade between them? What are the reasons for international trade? The theory of comparative costs, also known as comparative advantage, was formulated by David Ricardo around 1815. It is one of the oldest, still unchallenged theories of economics. S. Mill, Bastable, Marshall and Caimes introduced some changes but the final shape was given by Taussig, Heberler, Graham and Ohlin. This theory explains the existence of the direction of international or inter-regional trade. The classical theory of international trade was first stated by Adam Smith in the 18th century.

## 2.1. Theory of Absolute Cost Advantage :

The Scottish economist Adam Smith developed the trade theory of absolute advantage in 1776. A country that has an absolute advantage produces greater output of a good or service than other countries using the same amount of resources. Smith stated that tariffs and quotas should not restrict international trade; it should be allowed to flow according to market forces. Contrary to mercantilism, Smith argued that a country should concentrate on production of goods in which it holds an absolute advantage. No country would then need to produce all the goods it consumed. The theory of absolute advantage destroys the mercantilist idea that international trade is a zero-sum game.

According to the absolute advantage theory, international trade is a positive-sum game because there are gains for both countries to an exchange. Unlike mercantilism, this theory measures the nation's wealth by the living standards of its people and not by gold and silver. There is a potential problem with absolute advantage. If there is one country that does not have an absolute advantage in the production of any product, will there still be benefit to trade and will trade even occur? The answer may be found in the extension of absolute advantage, the theory of comparative advantage.

### 2.1.1. Meaning of Absolute Cost Advantage :

Absolute advantage is the ability of a country, individual, company or region to produce a goods or services at a lower cost per unit than the cost at which any other entity produces those goods or services. Absolute Advantage Entities with absolute advantages can produce something using a smaller number of inputs than another company producing the same product. As such, absolute advantage can reduce costs and boost profits. Since absolute advantage is determined by a simple comparison of labour productivities, it is possible for a party to have no absolute advantage in anything; in that case, according to the theory of absolute advantage, no trade will occur with the other party. It can be contrasted with the concept of comparative advantage which refers to the ability to produce a particular good at a lower opportunity cost.

### 2.1.2. Origin of Absolute Cost Advantage :

The main concept of absolute advantage is generally attributed to Adam Smith for his 1776 publication. An inquiry into the Nature and Causes of the Wealth of Nations in which he countered mercantilist ideas. Smith argued that it was impossible for all nations to become rich simultaneously by following mercantilism because the export of one nation is another nation's import and instead stated that all nations would gain simultaneously if they practiced free trade and specialised in accordance with their absolute advantage.

### 2.1.3. Background of Absolute Cost Advantage :

In the second half of the 18$^{th}$ century, mercantilist policies became an obstacle for the economic progress. Adam Smith (father of liberalism and economical science) brought the argument in his book "The Wealth of Nations", published in 1776, that the mercantilist policies favourite producers and disadvantaged the interests of consumers. Adam Smith's theory starts with the idea that export is profitable if you can import goods that could satisfy better the necessities of consumers instead of producing them on the internal market. The essence of Adam Smith theory is that the rule that leads the exchanges from any market, internal or external, is to determine the value of goods by measuring the labour incorporated in them.

### 2.1.4. Assumptions of Absolute Cost Advantage :

Adam Smith based his absolute cost advantage theory of international trade on the following assumptions:

1) Labour is the only factor of production and, therefore, exchange between goods was determined by the relative amounts of labour embodied in them.
2) There is full employment in the country.
3) Labour is mobile within the country but perfectly immobile between the countries.
4) The law of constant returns is in operation.

### 2.1.5. Complications and Limitations of Absolute Cost Advantage :

The Absolute Cost Advantage theory, also known as the theory of absolute advantage, was proposed by Adam Smith in the 18th century. It suggests that countries should specialize in producing goods or services in which they have an absolute cost advantage over other countries, and engage in international trade to maximize their welfare. While the theory has its merits, it also has certain limitations that should be considered. Some of the limitations of the Absolute Cost Advantage theory are as follows:

1) **Ignores Comparative Advantage:**
   The Absolute Cost Advantage theory focuses solely on the absolute cost of production, ignoring the concept of comparative advantage. Comparative advantage considers the opportunity cost of producing a good or service, taking into account the relative efficiency of production. By disregarding comparative advantage, the theory fails to capture the potential gains from trade based on specialization in goods or services with the lowest opportunity cost.
2) **Narrow Focus on Labor Productivity:**
   The theory primarily emphasizes labor productivity as the sole determinant of absolute cost advantage. It assumes that differences in labor productivity across countries are the main drivers of comparative advantage. However, other factors, such as natural resources, technology, capital, and institutional factors, can also play significant roles in determining a country's comparative advantage. By overlooking these factors, the theory provides a limited understanding of the complexities of international trade.
3) **Static Analysis:**
   The Absolute Cost Advantage theory assumes a static analysis of trade patterns and does not consider dynamic factors such as technological progress, changes in factor endowments, and economies of scale. In reality, these dynamic factors can significantly influence a country's comparative advantage and trade patterns over time. Failing to account for dynamic changes restricts the theory's applicability to the real world.

**4) Lack of Real-World Assumptions:**

The theory assumes a simplified world with perfect competition, full employment, absence of transaction costs, and no barriers to trade. However, in the real world, these assumptions rarely hold. Trade barriers, such as tariffs, quotas, and non-tariff barriers, significantly impact trade patterns. Transaction costs, including transportation, information, and legal costs, also affect trade flows. The theory's failure to incorporate these real-world assumptions limits its practical relevance.

**5) Inability to Explain Intraindustry Trade:**

The Absolute Cost Advantage theory struggles to explain intraindustry trade, where countries engage in simultaneous imports and exports of similar goods within the same industry. In the modern global economy, intraindustry trade is prevalent, and the theory's focus on absolute cost differences does not adequately capture the complexities of this type of trade.

**6) Ignores Distributional Consequences:**

The theory primarily focuses on overall efficiency gains from trade but overlooks the distributional consequences within countries. International trade can lead to winners and losers within economies, with certain industries and workers experiencing dislocation and job displacement. The theory's failure to address the distributional implications of trade limits its ability to provide a comprehensive analysis of the impact of trade on welfare.

**7) Lack of Consideration for Non-Price Factors:**

The Absolute Cost Advantage theory primarily emphasizes price differentials as the basis for trade patterns. However, there are numerous non-price factors that can influence trade, such as product differentiation, brand reputation, quality standards, and customer preferences. These non-price factors can give rise to trade patterns that are not solely determined by absolute cost advantages.

**8) Absence of Absolute Advantage :**

The example discusses a situation where one country has an absolute advantage in the production of one good and the other country in the production of another good. It is frequently argued that developing countries may lack the technology to gain an absolute advantage in the production of any good such that they cannot possibly compete on the global market and benefit from free trade. This conclusion is wrong as analysed in the Ricardian model (comparative advantage) since technologically disadvantaged countries can compete on the global market by paying lower wages. It turns out that absolute advantage is neither a necessary nor a sufficient condition for exporting a certain good and gain from international trade.

**9) More Factors of Production :**

In reality, goods are produced using several factors of production simultaneously such as capital, land and various types of labour. Usually, goods then cannot be ranked according to absolute advantage as their production in one country requires more of one input and simultaneously less of another input than in another country. These issues are analysed in the Heckscher-Ohlin (factor abundance) theory of international trade.

**10) Intra versus Inter-industry Trade :**

The example discusses inter-industry trade which is the exchange of one type of good (cars) for another type of good (food). Many countries engage in intra-industry trade, the exchange of similar types of goods (e.g. simultaneously exporting and importing car parts). This type of trade is becoming ever more important. It can be based on market power and economies of scale as analysed in new trade theory.

## 2.2. Theory of Comparative Cost Advantage :

The most basic concept in the whole of international trade theory is the principle of comparative advantage, first introduced by David Ricardo in 1817. It remains a major influence on much international trade policy and is, therefore, important in understanding the modern global economy. The principle of comparative advantage states that a country should specialise in producing and exporting those products in which it has a comparative or relative cost, advantage compared with other countries and should import those goods in which it has a comparative disadvantage.

### 2.2.1. Meaning of Comparative Cost Advantage :

The ability of a firm or individual is to produce goods and/or services at a lower opportunity cost than other firms or individuals. A comparative advantage gives a company the ability to sell goods and services at a lower price than its competitors and realise stronger sales margins. Comparative Advantage having a comparative advantage or disadvantage can shape a company's entire focus. For example, if a cruise company found that had a comparative advantage over a similar company, due to its closer proximity to a port, it might encourage the latter to focus on other, more productive, aspects of countries.

### 2.2.2. Origin of Comparative Cost Advantage :

The idea of comparative advantage has been first mentioned in Adam Smith's Book the "Wealth of Nations". "If a foreign country can supply us with a commodity cheaper than we ourselves can make it, better buy it of them with some part of the produce of our own industry, employed in a way in which we have some advantage." But the law of comparative advantages has been formulated by David Ricardo who investigated in detail advantages and alternative or relative opportunity in his 1817 book 'On the Principles of political Economy and Taxation' in an example involving England and Portugal.

## 2.2.3. Richardo's Theory of Comparative Cost Advantage Assumptions :

Ricardo explains his theory with the help of following assumptions:

1) There are two countries and two commodities.
2) There is a perfect competition both in commodity and factor market.
3) Cost of production is expressed in terms of labour i.e. value of a commodity is measured in terms of labour hours/days required to produce it. Commodities are also exchanged on the basis of labour content of each good.
4) Labour is the only factor of production other than natural resources.
5) Labour is homogeneous i.e. identical in efficiency in a particular country.
6) Labour is perfectly mobile within a country but perfectly immobile between countries.
7) There is free trade i.e. the movement of goods between countries is not hindered by any restrictions.
8) Production is subject to constant returns to scale.
9) There is no technological change.
10) Trade between two countries takes place on barter system.
11) Full employment exists in both countries.
12) Perfect occupational mobility of factors of production - resources used in one industry can be switched into another without any loss of efficiency.
13) Perfect occupational mobility of factors of production - resources used in one industry can be switched into another without any loss of efficiency.
14) Constant returns to scale (i.e. doubling the inputs in each country leads to a doubling of total output).
15) No externalities arising from production and/or consumption.
16) Transportation costs are ignored.
17) If businesses exploit increasing returns to scale (i.e. economies of scale) when they specialise, the potential gains from trade are much greater.

    The idea that specialisation should lead to increasing returns is associated with economists such as Paul Romer and Paul Ormerod.

## 2.2.4. Determinants of Comparative Cost Advantage :

Comparative advantage is a dynamic concept. It can and does change over time. Some businesses find that they have enjoyed a comparative advantage in one product for several years only to face increasing competition as rival producers from other countries enter their markets. For a country, the following factors are important in determining the relative costs of production:

1) **The Quantity and Quality of Factors of Production available :**

    If an economy can improve the quality of its labour force and increase the stock of capital available; it can expand the productive potential in industries in which it has an advantage.

2) **Investment in Research and Development :**
Important in industries where patents give some firms significant market advantage an appreciation of the exchange rate can cause exports from a country to increase in price. This makes them less competitive in international markets.

3) **Long-term Rates of Inflation Compared to other Countries :**
For example if average inflation in Country X is 4% whilst in Country B, it is 8% over a number of years, the goods and services produced by Country X will become relatively more expensive over time. This worsens their competitiveness and causes a switch in comparative advantage.

4) **Import Controls like Tariffs and Quotas :**
Import controls such as tariffs and quotas that can be used to create an artificial comparative advantage for a country's domestic producers - although most countries agree to abide by international trade agreements.

### 2.2.5. Considerations of Ricardo's Theory of Comparative Advantage :

The considerations for Ricardo's theory are as follows:

1) **Development Economics :**
The theory of comparative advantage and the corollary that nations should specialise, is criticised on pragmatic grounds within the import substitution industrialisation theory of development economics, on empirical grounds by the Singer Prussia thesis which states that terms of trade between primary producers and manufactured goods deteriorate over time and on theoretical grounds of infant industry and Keynesian economics. In older economic terms, comparative advantage has been opposed by mercantilism and economic nationalism.

2) **Free Mobility of Capital in a Globalise World :**
Ricardo explicitly bases his argument on an assumed immobility of capital "if capital freely flowed towards those countries where it could be most profitably employed, there could be no difference in the rate of profit and no other difference in the real or labour price of commodities than the additional quantity of labour required to convey them to the various markets where they were to be sold."

### 2.2.6. Criticisms of Theory of Comparative Advantage :

The theory of comparative advantage, first introduced by David Ricardo in the early 19th century, is a fundamental concept in international trade. It suggests that countries should specialize in producing goods or services in which they have a lower opportunity cost compared to other countries, and engage in trade to maximize overall welfare. While the theory has been widely accepted and has provided valuable insights into international trade patterns, it is not without its criticisms. In following discussion, we will explore some of the main criticisms of the theory of comparative advantage.

1) **Static Analysis:**
One common criticism of the theory of comparative advantage is that it relies on a static analysis of trade patterns. It assumes that comparative advantage is constant over time, ignoring the potential for dynamic changes in a country's advantage. In reality, comparative advantage can change due to factors such as technological progress, changes in factor endowments, and economies of scale. By not accounting for these dynamic factors, the theory fails to capture the evolving nature of comparative advantage in the real world.

2) **Unrealistic Assumptions:**
The theory of comparative advantage relies on several simplifying assumptions that may not hold in reality. For instance, it assumes that there are no transportation costs, no trade barriers, perfect competition, and full employment of resources. In practice, these assumptions do not align with the complexities of the global economy. Trade barriers, such as tariffs and non-tariff barriers, significantly affect trade patterns, and transportation costs can impact the comparative advantage of certain goods. Furthermore, imperfect competition and labor market frictions can lead to inefficiencies and distortions in trade.

3) **Narrow Focus on Labor Productivity:**
The theory of comparative advantage predominantly focuses on differences in labor productivity as the main determinant of comparative advantage. It assumes that countries differ only in terms of labor efficiency. However, other factors, such as capital, technology, natural resources, and institutional factors, also play crucial roles in determining a country's comparative advantage. Ignoring these factors limits the theory's ability to explain the complexity of trade patterns in the real world.

4) **Inability to Address Distributional Consequences:**
Another criticism of the theory of comparative advantage is its limited consideration of the distributional consequences of trade. While the theory suggests that trade leads to overall welfare gains, it fails to address how the gains from trade are distributed within countries. International trade can result in winners and losers, as certain industries may face job losses or face difficulties adjusting to increased import competition. The theory's focus on aggregate welfare obscures the potential distributional impacts of trade, which can have important social and political implications.

5) **Disregard for Non-economic Factors:**
The theory of comparative advantage primarily focuses on economic factors and assumes that trade is solely determined by differences in production costs. However, trade patterns can also be influenced by non-economic factors such as cultural preferences, historical ties, political considerations, and government policies. For example, countries may choose to protect certain industries for national security reasons or to maintain strategic autonomy. By neglecting these

non-economic factors, the theory provides an incomplete understanding of trade patterns.

6) **Failure to Explain Intraindustry Trade:**
The theory of comparative advantage struggles to explain intraindustry trade, where countries engage in simultaneous imports and exports of similar goods within the same industry. In the modern global economy, intraindustry trade is common, as countries specialize in producing different varieties or qualities of a particular good. The theory's focus on absolute cost differences fails to capture the complexity of intraindustry trade and the role of product differentiation, branding, and quality standards.

7) **Ignoring Environmental and Social Externalities:**
The theory of comparative advantage does not account for environmental and social externalities associated with trade. It assumes that the pursuit of comparative advantage will lead to efficient outcomes without considering the potential negative impacts on the environment or labor standards. For instance, countries with lax environmental regulations may gain a comparative advantage in industries that generate pollution. This omission limits the theory's ability to address sustainability concerns and the need for policy interventions to address externalities.

8) **Lack of Factor Mobility:**
The theory of comparative advantage assumes that factors of production are immobile between countries. However, in reality, factors such as capital and labor can move across borders. The theory does not fully account for the implications of factor mobility on trade patterns and the distribution of gains from trade.

9) **Inequality and Terms of Trade:**
The theory of comparative advantage assumes that trade is based on voluntary exchange and mutually beneficial terms. However, in practice, power dynamics, information asymmetry, and unequal bargaining positions can result in unequal terms of trade. Less developed countries may find themselves in a disadvantageous position, facing exploitation and unequal exchange in international trade.

10) **Shortcomings in the Measurement of Comparative Advantage:**
The measurement of comparative advantage can be challenging in practice. The theory relies on the concept of opportunity cost, which is difficult to quantify accurately. It requires assumptions about production functions, input-output relationships, and the measurement of prices and wages. These measurement issues can limit the practical application of the theory and its ability to provide precise policy recommendations.

11) **Ohlin's Criticism:**
Professor Bertil Ohlin objects to the theory of comparative costs as an explanation of international trade, for, in his view, the comparative cost principle was applicable to all trade and that international trade was no exception to it.

He thus regards the classical doctrine of comparative costs as a clumsy and dangerous tool of analysis. It is also unrealistic as it considers only a two-country, two-commodity phenomenon based on the labour theory of value. Hence, Ohlin propounded a new theory of international trade based on the general theory of value. Despite these limitations, the theory has a stand. It has narrated the truth that comparative advantage is definitely an advantage which should be gainfully exploited in international trade. To quote Professor Samuelson, "Whether or not one of two regions is absolutely more efficient in the production of every good than is the other, if each specialise in the products in which it has a comparative advantage (greater relative efficiency), trade will be mutually profitable to both regions.

Real wage of productive factors will rise in both places." He also appreciates Ricardo's presumption of free trade policy and writes, "An ill-designed probability tariff or quota, far from helping the protected factor of production, will instead reduce its real wage by making imports expensive and by making the whole world less productive through eliminating the efficiency inherent in the best pattern of specialisation and division of labour." Indeed, in this way, the doctrine of comparative advantage does provide an unshakeable basis for international trade.

## 2.3. Heckscher- Ohlin Theory:

As a matter of fact, Ohlin's theory begins where the Ricardian theory of international trade ends. The Ricardian theory states that the basis of international trade is the comparative costs difference. But he did not explain how after all this comparative costs difference arises. Ohlin's theory explains the real cause of this difference. Ohlin did not invalidate the classical theory but accepted the comparative advantage as the cause of international trade and then tried to examine and analyse it further in a moral and logical manner. Thus, Ohlin's theory supplements but does not supplant the Ricardian theory. Ohlin states that trade results on account of the different relative price of different goods in different countries. The relative price commodity difference is the result of relative costs and factor price differences in different countries. Differences in factor prices are due to differences in factor endowments in different countries. It, thus, boils down to the fact that trade occurs because different countries have different factor endowments. Ohlin's theory is, therefore, also described as the factor endowment theory or the factor proportions analysis. Ohlin's theory is usually expounded in terms of a two-factor model with labour and capital as the two factors of endowments.

### 2.3.1. Definition of Heckscher- Ohlin Theory :

"The Heckscher-Ohlin Theory states that difference in relative factor endowments and factor prices between nations is the most important cause of trade. This theory predicts that each nation will export the commodity in the production of which a great deal of relatively abundant and cheap factor is used and import the commodity in the production of which a great deal of its relatively scarce and expensive factor is used. The theory also predicts that trade will lead to the reduction in the difference in factor prices between nations."

## 2.3.2. Assumptions of Heckscher- Ohlin Theory :

Following are the assumptions of factor Endowment Hecksherohin Theory:

1) This theory relates to two countries, two commodities and two factors. It is, therefore, called 2 X 2 X 2 model.
2) There is same production function for each commodity in two countries.
3) Factors are mobile within the country but immobile between two countries.
4) There is perfect competition in all markets. As a result (a) all factors are fully employed (b) factors get their reward in accordance with their marginal productivity (c) prices of the commodities are equal to their marginal productivity.
5) No restriction is imposed on the exchange of goods i.e. free trade exists between two countries.
6) Consumer's tastes and preferences are identical in two countries.
7) Technique of production employed in two countries is the same.
8) There is lack of transport costs.
9) Factor endowments are different in two countries.
10) Goods can be classified on the basis of factor intensity such as capital intensive goods and labour intensive goods etc.
11) Production functions are homogenous of the first degree. It implies that if factors of production are doubled, the production too will be doubled.

## 2.3.3. Explanation of Heckscher- Ohlin Theory :

According to Ohlin *"International Trade is but a special case of inter-regional trade."* Different regions have different factor endowments, that is, some regions have abundance of labour but scarcity of capital while other regions have abundance of capital but scarcity of labour. Different goods have different production function, that is, factors are combined in different proportions to produce different commodities. Some goods are produced by employing relatively large proportion of labour and relatively small proportion of capital. Still other goods are produced by employing relatively small proportion of labour and relatively large proportion of capital. In this way, each region is suitable for the production of those goods for whose production it has relatively abundant supply of the required factors. A region is not suitable for the production of those goods for whose production it has relatively scarce or zero supply of the essential factors. Hence, different regions have different capacity to produce different commodities, difference in factor endowments is, therefore, the main cause of international trade along with inter- regional trade.

According to Ohlin, "Immediate cause of inter-regional trade is always that 90% can be bought cheaper in terms of money than they can be produced at home and here is the case of international trade. Heckscher in his article “The effect of Foreign Trade on the Distribution of income” published in 1919 had supported the classical theory of Comparative Costs and maintained that international trade took place cause of differences in comparative costs. But classical theory did not explain why there was a difference in comparative cost. Heckscher states the following causes for difference in comparative costs:

1) Difference in Factor Endowments.
2) Difference in Factor Intensities.

According to Heckscher Ohlin Theory of International Trade, the immediate cause of International trade is the difference in relative commodity prices. The cause of differ; hence, in the relative prices of the goods is the difference in the amount of factor endowments like capital and labour between the two countries. As a result, there is difference in the relative demand and supply of factors. These differences cause difference in the prices of the factors. It is due to difference in factor prices that difference in the relative prices of the commodities takes place and it is this difference that constitutes the main cause of international trade. Goods which require scarce factors on a large-scale are imported because their domestic prices are high. On the contrary, goods which require abundant factors on a large scale are exported as their domestic prices are low. For instance, if capital is abundant in Germany, it will be relatively cheap. Hence, Germany will export those goods which are capital intensive. On the contrary, if labour is abundant in India, it will be relatively cheap. Hence, India will export those goods which are labour intensive. Abundance or scarcity of factors of Heckscher-Ohlin theory has been explained on the basis of two criteria: (i) Price Criterion and (ii) Physical Criterion. Heckscher-Ohlin theory can explain on the basis of these two criteria.

a) **Price Criterion of Factor Abundance or Scarcity :**

   Price criterion of factor abundance or scarcity means that countries where capital is relatively cheap and labour relatively clear, will be called capital abundant country even if the quantity of capital in that country is relatively less. On the contrary, if capital B relatively clear and labour relatively cheap such a country will be called capital scarce country even if the quantity of capital in such a country is relatively more. In other words, the criterion of factor abundance or factor scarcity is not the quantum of the factor but its price. On the basis of price criterion, international trade theory can be explained with the help of an example.

b) **Diagrammatic Explanation :**

   Let us take Germany and India as are two trading countries. It is assumed that Germany is a capital intensive country and India is a labour intensive country. So that capital is cheaper in Germany in relation to labour and labour is cheaper in India in relation to capital. This can be expressed in terms of the following equation:

$$\underset{\text{Germany}}{\left(\frac{P_K}{P_L}\right)} < \underset{\text{India}}{\left(\frac{P_K}{P_L}\right)}$$

Here, PK: price of capital; PL: price of labour; <: less than.

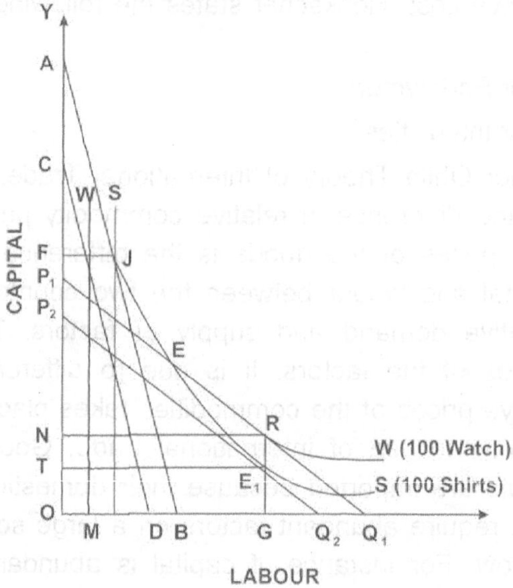


Both the countries are producing watches and shirts. While the production of watches is capital intensive, the production of shirts is labour intensive. According to Heckscher- Ohlin theory, India should specialise in the production of shirts and Germany should specialise in the production of watches. This is illustrated in figure. In this figure, labour is shown on the X-axis and capital is shown on the Y axis. WW, 100 is isoquant showing production of 100 watches and SS, 100 is the isoquant showing production of 100 shirts. AB and CD are iso cost lines for Germany. These are parallel straight lines which mean their slope is same and, (since slope shows price ratio) these iso cost lines are showing the same price ratio. Thus,

$$\frac{OA}{OB} = \frac{OC}{OD}$$

These iso-cost lines are inclined towards OY axis showing that in Germany, capital is cheaper in relation to labour. Likewise P1 Q1 and P2 Q2 are iso cost lines for India. These are inclined towards OX-axis showing that, in India, labour is cheaper in relation to capital. These lines are also parallel. So that these are showing the same price ratio.

$$\frac{OP_1}{OQ_1} = \frac{OP_2}{OQ_2}$$

Isoquants WW and SS are intersecting each other only at point E. This implies that there is no reversal of factor intensity. Or that in both Germany and India, production of watches is capital intensive and production of shirts is labour intensive. This conclusion is based on the assumption of Heckscher-Ohlin theory that both in Germany and India, production function of watches or of shirts is similar. The diagram shows that, in case of Germany, iso-cost line CD and iso product curve WW for watches is tangent at point H. So that, for Germany,

Production Cost for 100 Watches = OF Capital + OM Labour

As regards the production of shirts, we find iso-cost line AB and iso-product curve SS are tangent at point J. So that for Germany,

Production Cost of 100 shirts = OF Capital + OM1 Labour

In Germany, capital cost of production of watches or of shirts is equal to OF but labour cost of shirts is OM1. While labour cost of watches is OM.

Implying that labour cost of shirts is more by MM1 (OM1- OM = MM1) units of labour.

Thus, Germany can produce watches at relatively lesser cost compared to the production of shirts. In case of India, iso cost line P1Q1 and is product curve WW for watches are tangent at point R. So that, for India.

Product Cost of 100 Watches = ON Capital + OG Labour

Likewise iso cost line P2 O2 and iso product curve SS for shirts are tangent at point E1.

So that,

Product Cost of 100 Shirts = OT Capital + OG Labour

Thus, in India, labour cost of watches and shirts = OG but capital cost of shirts is less than the capital cost of watches by NT capital (ON - OT = NT). This suggests that India can produce shirts at lesser cost compared to watches. So that India should specialise in the production of shirts and export the same.

It is, thus, suggested that because capital is relatively cheaper in Germany and because labour is relatively cheaper in India, Germany should specialise in the production of capital-intensive goods i.e. watches and India should specialise in the production of labour-intensive goods i.e. shirts. Germany will export watches.

**Physical Criterion of Factor Abundance or Scarcity:**

Physical criterion of factor abundance or scarcity means that if in a country, capital ratio is greater than labour as against another country then it will be called capital intensive country. Likewise if in a country, labour ratio is greater than capital as against another country then it will be called labour intensive country.

In other words, basis of this criterion is the physical quantity of the factors. On the basis of this criterion, international trade can be explained with the help of the following example.

**Example:** According to Heckscher-Ohlin whether two countries, say Germany and India, are capital intensive or labour intensive depends on the fulfillment of the following condition: $\frac{K_G}{L_G} > \frac{K_1}{L_1}$

(Here KG = Quantity of Capital in Germany; LG = Quantity of Labour in Germany; K1 = Quantity of Capital in India; L1 = Quantity of Labour in India)

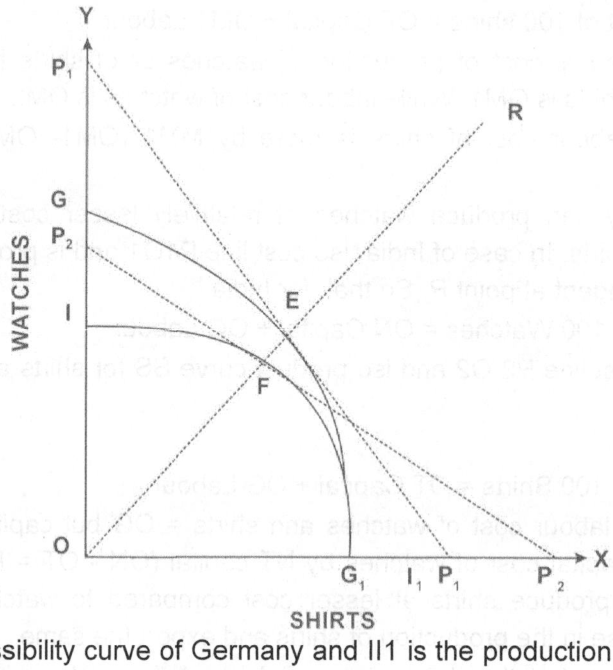


Production possibility curve of Germany and II1 is the production possibility curve of India. Labour intensive production i.e. shirts is shown on OX-axis and capital intensive production i.e. watches is shown on OY- axis. If both the countries produce both the goods in the same ratio then they will produce along OR-ray. Germany will produce at point E of its production possibility curve GG1 and India will produce at point F of its production possibility curve II1. It is evident from this figure that at point E, the slope of production possibility curve of Germany is steeper and at point F while the slope of production possibility curve of India is flatter. It is clear from the fact that P1P1 price line of Germany is steeper than P2P2 price line of India. It proves that watches are cheaper in Germany and shirts are cheaper in India. Germany should produce more of capital intensive goods viz. watches. It may, however, be noted that the above analysis does not clarify whether Germany will export watches and India shirts. Answer to this question depends on the demand for these goods. If the domestic demand of Germany for watches is less than the supply then alone it will export watches otherwise not. Likewise, India too will export shirts only if domestic demand for shirts is less than the supply.

### 2.3.4. Critiques the of Heckscher- Ohlin Theory :

The Heckscher-Ohlin theory, also known as the factor proportions theory, is a fundamental concept in international trade. It suggests that countries will specialize in and export goods that use their abundant factors of production relatively intensively, while importing goods that use their scarce factors of production intensively. While the theory has made significant contributions to our understanding of international trade patterns, it is not without its critiques. In following discussion, we will explore some of the main criticisms of the Heckscher-Ohlin theory.

1) **Simplistic Assumptions:**
   The Heckscher-Ohlin theory relies on several simplifying assumptions that may not hold in reality. For instance, it assumes that there are only two factors of production (capital and labor), two goods, and constant returns to scale. In reality, there are other factors such as land, natural resources, and technology that can significantly influence trade patterns. Additionally, constant returns to scale may not accurately capture the complexities of production processes and economies of scale.
2) **Lack of Factor Mobility:**
   The theory assumes that factors of production are immobile between countries, meaning that capital and labor cannot move freely across borders. In reality, there is varying degrees of factor mobility, including the movement of capital and skilled labor. The failure to account for factor mobility limits the theory's ability to explain real-world trade patterns and the distributional consequences of trade.
3) **Non-Homogeneous Factors:**
   The Heckscher-Ohlin theory assumes that factors of production is homogeneous within a country but differ in relative abundance across countries. However, in reality, factors such as labor and capital can be diverse in terms of skills, education, and technological capabilities. Ignoring these differences can result in oversimplifications and inaccuracies in predicting trade patterns.
4) **Incomplete Explanation of Trade:**
   The Heckscher-Ohlin theory focuses primarily on the role of factor endowments in determining trade patterns. It does not fully consider other factors such as technology, product differentiation, economies of scale, and non-price factors that influence trade. This limitation hinders the theory's ability to provide a comprehensive explanation of trade patterns, especially in cases of intraindustry trade where countries specialize in producing different varieties or qualities of a particular good.

5) **Dynamic Considerations:**

The theory assumes a static analysis and does not account for dynamic changes over time, such as technological progress, changes in factor endowments, and shifts in comparative advantage. In reality, these dynamic factors can significantly impact trade patterns, and the theory fails to capture the complexities of these adjustments.

6) **Limited Scope for Trade:**

The Heckscher-Ohlin theory suggests that trade is driven solely by factor endowments, limiting the scope for other determinants of trade, such as economies of scale, technological differences, and firm-level competitiveness. By focusing solely on factor endowments, the theory overlooks the richness of trade dynamics and the diverse factors that influence comparative advantage.

7) **Distributional Implications:**

While the Heckscher-Ohlin theory acknowledges that trade can lead to overall welfare gains, it does not fully address the distributional consequences within countries. Trade can lead to winners and losers, with certain industries or workers facing dislocation or job displacement. The theory's emphasis on aggregate welfare gains obscures the potential inequality and social implications of trade.

8) **Limited Predictive Power:**

The Heckscher-Ohlin theory has faced challenges in its empirical verification and predictive power. The theory's assumptions and simplified framework may not fully capture the complexities of real-world trade patterns. Empirical studies have shown that factors other than factor endowments, such as productivity differences, trade costs, and institutional factors, also play significant roles in shaping trade patterns.

9) **Failure to Explain Intra-Industry Trade:**

The Heckscher-Ohlin theory struggles to explain intraindustry trade, where countries simultaneously import and export similar goods within the same industry. The theory's focus on factor endowments and comparative advantage does not adequately capture the complexities of intraindustry trade and the role of product differentiation, specialization, and economies of scale.

10) **Lack of Policy Prescriptions:**

The Heckscher-Ohlin theory does not provide clear policy prescriptions for countries to improve their welfare through trade. The theory primarily focuses on the allocation of resources based on comparative advantage but does not offer guidance on how to enhance factor endowments, improve productivity, or address distributional consequences.

## 2.4. Leontief's Paradox :

In 1953, Wassily Leontief published a study named, "Domestic production and foreign trade: the American capital position re-examined" where he tested the validity of the

Heckscher-Ohlin theory. Using data available from the 1947 input-output (I-O) model of the US economy, Leontief calculated the K and L requirements for the production of $1 million of US exports and $1 million of US production in import-competing industries. He found that the former required a higher proportion of L than the latter. The study showed that the U.S. was more abundant in capital compared to other countries; therefore, the U.S. would export capital - intensive goods and import labour-intensive goods. Leontief found out that the U.S.'s export was less capital intensive than import. Hecksher-Ohlin's theory of factor endowments stressed that a country should produce and export goods that require resources (factors) that are abundant in the home country. Leontief tested the Hecksher-Ohlin theory in the U.S. and found that it was not applicable in the U.S.

### 2.4.1. Meaning of the Leontief Paradox :

An essential part of the Heckscher-Ohlin theory is the assumptions of identical production functions and absence of reversibility of factor intensities for different commodities. The assumption of identical production functions implies apart from identical knowledge, skills and so forth, also identical climates, physical and social milieu and so on. Ohlin thought it self-evident that the production function is everywhere the same. It followed, in his opinion, from the fact that the same causes produce everywhere (and at every time) the same effects. "The constancy of the laws of nature" must ensure identical production functions between different countries. However, to be meaningful, the concept of the production function should be conceived in terms of the well-defined variable inputs leaving a milieu and climate factors extra curriculum outside the function.

### 2.4.2. Background of Leontief Paradox :

The most comprehensive empirical work done to examine the influence of factor endowment on international trade in the general framework of the Heckscher-Ohlin trade model was done by Leontief who constructed an input-output table for the United States based on 1947, data for 192 industries. He computed the requirements for one million dollar worth of exports for 1947 and the US production of one million dollar worth of import replacements. He found that in 1947, the USA apparently exported labour-intensive goods and imported capital-intensive ones. According to Leontief, the US export industries used relatively more labour than did the import-competing industries as expressed by the following figures.

**Per Million Dollars:**

| Particular Exports Import | Import | Replacements |
|---|---|---|
| Capital (dollars in 1947 prices) | 2,550,780 | 3,091,337 |
| (Labour (man-years)) | 182,313 | 170004 |

Thus, American import-replacement industries required more capital to labour than did the American export industries. Even after a more extensive and detailed enquiry conducted in part on 1951 data, as well as data for 1947, Leontief saw no reason whatever for changing this conclusion.

### 2.4.3. Leontief's Theory Explanation :

Leontief himself tried to resolve the paradox by giving different explanations. He always kept two things in mind. Firstly, to rescue the Heckscher-Ohlin theory from apparent refutation. Secondly, the common belief that America has more capital per worker than any other country. Leontief's different explanation mainly ran along two different lines.

1) **Safeguard of the Validity of the Heckscher-Ohlin Theory :**
   Leontief gave priority to labour efficiency (productivity) and argued that the American worker was three times as efficient as was a worker elsewhere. Hence, the effective supply of labour in America must be regarded as a certain multiple of the apparent labour supply there. After adjusting for varying degrees of labour efficiency, America would be found to be relatively rich in labour and poor in capital.
2) **Explanation Connected with the Two-factor Framework and Broad Use of the Term Capital :**
   The only two factors considered in Leontief's study are labour and capital. Noting the inadequacy of his procedure Leontief himself observed, "Invisible in all these tables but ever present as a third factor or rather as whole additional set of factors determining this country's productive capacity, in particular, its comparative advantage vis-a-vis the rest of the world are natural resources, agricultural lands, forests, rivers and other rich mineral resources." An explanation of the paradox can be obtained if one takes into account this third factor. Though empirical research in this field is not conclusive, no other trade models have proved to be as effective in predicting the trade flows as either the classical or the Heckscher-Ohlin trade model.

### 2.4.4. Limitations of Leontief Paradox :

Limitations of Leontief Paradox are as following:

1) **Inadequate and Inappropriate :**
   Several writers have questioned the accuracy and appropriateness of the data.
2) **Not Logically Valid :**
   Several others have argued that Leontief's procedure is not logically valid method of testing the empirical validity of the Heckscher-Ohlin theory. For example, N.S. Buchanan criticised Leontief's measurement of capital. In his opinion, Leonitief's capital coefficients were investment requirement coefficients which did not take into account the durability of capital.

**3) Insignificant Differences :**

G.A. Loeb argues that differences in intensity between the export sector and the import-competing sectors were not statistically significant.

**4) Inappropriate Timing :**

B.C. Swerling argues that 1947, the year selected for his study by Leontief, was a typical year as far as trade flows were concerned.

**5) Inadequate Dealing with Natural Resources :**

Erik Hoffmeyer argues that the Leontief Paradox is due to Leontief's failure to deal adequately with natural resources. If commodities that require a relatively large amount of natural resources are excluded from the capital-labour ratios then Leontief's conclusion will be reversed and the paradox will disappear. As Leontief was concerned only with import replacements, it would be better to exclude from the calculations of those commodities which are intensive in natural resources.

**6) Wrong Comparison of Factor Intensities :**

P.T. Ellsworth suggested that the comparison of factor-intensities should be confined to the case of American imports and foreign exports and not as Leontief has done to the case of American exports and American import replacements. For the imports from each country of origin, he should have computed the capital-labour ratio on the basis of input-output studies of these economies. As Leontief has not done this, only half of Leontief's calculations, those relating to capital-labour ratio of American exports were relevant while those halves relating to the import replacements were irrelevant. However, most critics treat Ellsworth's argument against the basic postulates of the Heckscher-Ohlin theory which assumes that production functions are everywhere identical.

## 2.5. Rybczynski Theorem:

The Rybczynski theorem is an important concept in international trade theory that explores the relationship between factor endowments, production possibilities, and changes in the allocation of resources. It provides insights into how changes in the availability of factors of production, such as labor and capital, affect the production and trade patterns of a country.

The Rybczynski theorem, named after the economist Tadeusz Rybczynski, is an extension of the Heckscher-Ohlin model, which is a fundamental theory of international trade. The Heckscher-Ohlin model states that countries will specialize in and export goods that intensively use factors of production that they are relatively abundant in, and import goods that intensively use factors they are relatively scarce in. The Rybczynski theorem builds upon this framework by examining the effects of changes in factor endowments on the production and trade patterns of a country.

### 2.5.1 Assumptions of the Rybczynski Theorem:

To understand the Rybczynski theorem, it is important to consider the assumptions on which it is based. These assumptions include:

1) **Two Factors of Production:**
   The Rybczynski theorem assumes that production is determined by the quantities of two factors of production, typically capital (K) and labor (L). This assumption allows for a simplified analysis of the relationships between factor endowments, production possibilities, and trade.
2) **Fixed Technology:**
   The theorem assumes a fixed technology, meaning that the production techniques and methods do not change throughout the analysis. This assumption allows for a focus on the impact of changes in factor endowments on production and trade outcomes.
3) **Perfect Competition:**
   The Rybczynski theorem assumes perfect competition in both input and output markets. This assumption ensures that prices are determined by market forces and that firms maximize their profits.
4) **Constant Returns to Scale:**
   The theorem assumes constant returns to scale, meaning that a proportional increase in inputs will lead to an equal proportional increase in outputs. This assumption allows for a simplified analysis and facilitates the examination of the relationships between factor endowments and production possibilities.

### 2.5.2 Conceptual Framework and Mathematical Formulation:

The Rybczynski theorem explores the relationship between changes in factor endowments and changes in the production and trade patterns of a country. It demonstrates how an increase in the availability of a factor of production, such as labor or capital, will affect the output levels of different goods.

To illustrate the theorem, let's consider a simple two-sector economy that produces two goods, X and Y, using capital (K) and labor (L) as factors of production. Initially, the economy is in equilibrium, producing a certain quantity of each good, given the existing factor endowments and technology.

The Rybczynski theorem focuses on changes in factor endowments. Let's assume there is an exogenous increase in the endowment of one factor, for example, an increase in the supply of labor (L). This increase in the labor endowment will lead to a reallocation of resources and affect the production and trade patterns of the economy.

To understand the impact of the change in factor endowment, we need to examine the relationship between factor inputs and output quantities. The production functions for goods X and Y can be represented as follows:

$X = f(K, L)$

$Y = g(K, L)$

Where f (K, L) and g (K, L) are production functions that describe how outputs (X and Y) depend on inputs (K and L).

The Rybczynski theorem states that an increase in the endowment of a factor of production will lead to an expansion of output in the sector that uses the augmented factor more intensively, while output in the other sector will contract.

Mathematically, we can express the effects of changes in factor endowments using partial derivatives. The theorem can be represented as:

$(\partial X/\partial L) > 0$ and $(\partial Y/\partial L) < 0$

$(\partial X/\partial K) < 0$ and $(\partial Y/\partial K) > 0$

This implies that when the labor endowment increases ($\partial L > 0$), the output of good X will increase ($\partial X > 0$), and the output of good Y will decrease ($\partial Y < 0$). Conversely, when the capital endowment increases ($\partial K > 0$), the output of good X will decrease ($\partial X < 0$), and the output of good Y will increase ($\partial Y > 0$).

The theorem suggests that changes in factor endowments will cause a relative expansion or contraction of goods depending on their factor intensity. Goods that are more labor-intensive will experience a larger increase in output when the labor endowment expands, while goods that are more capital-intensive will experience a larger increase in output when the capital endowment expands.

## 2.5.3 Implications of the Rybczynski Theorem:

The Rybczynski theorem has several important implications for international trade:

1) **Trade and Factor Endowments:**
   The theorem suggests that changes in factor endowments can drive changes in the production and trade patterns of a country. An increase in the endowment of a factor will lead to a greater production of the good that uses that factor more intensively and a decline in the production of the other good.
2) **Impact on Relative Prices:**
   The Rybczynski theorem also has implications for relative prices. An increase in the supply of a factor will lower its relative price due to the expanded output in the sector using that factor more intensively. Conversely, the relative price of the other factor will increase due to the contraction in its production.
3) **Trade and Factor Mobility:**
   The theorem suggests that changes in factor endowments can be an important driver of international trade. If factor endowments change differently across countries, it can lead to differences in comparative advantage and specialization patterns, motivating trade between countries.

4) **Factor Substitution:**
The Rybczynski theorem implies that changes in factor endowments will lead to changes in the allocation of factors between sectors. As one factor becomes relatively more abundant, it will be substituted for the other factor, given their different factor intensities across sectors.

## 2.5.4 Limitations of the Rybczynski Theorem:

While the Rybczynski theorem provides valuable insights into the relationship between factor endowments and production patterns, it also has some limitations:

1) **Simplified Assumptions:**
The theorem relies on several simplifying assumptions, such as fixed technology, perfect competition, and constant returns to scale. These assumptions may not hold in the real world, limiting the generalizability of the theorem's findings.

2) **Single Factor Change:**
The theorem focuses on the impact of a single factor endowment change at a time. In reality, changes in factor endowments are often intertwined, and multiple factors may change simultaneously, making the analysis more complex.

3) **Factors Beyond Labor and Capital:**
The Rybczynski theorem assumes that production is determined solely by labor and capital. In reality, there are other factors of production, such as land, natural resources, and technology that can significantly influence production and trade patterns.

4) **Dynamic Considerations:**
The theorem analyzes the static effects of changes in factor endowments on production and trade patterns. It does not account for the dynamic adjustments that may occur over time, such as investment, technological progress, and changes in factor prices.

## 2.5.5 Real-World Examples and Empirical Evidence:

Empirical studies have examined the implications of the Rybczynski theorem using real-world data. For example, researchers have analyzed the effects of changes in labor endowments on the production and trade patterns of countries.

One study by Robert Baldwin and co-authors investigated the impact of changes in labor endowments on U.S. trade patterns with Mexico and other countries. They found empirical evidence supporting the predictions of the Rybczynski theorem, showing that an increase in labor endowments in Mexico led to an expansion of labor-intensive goods exports to the U.S.

Other studies have examined the implications of the Rybczynski theorem in different contexts and sectors, providing further support for the theorem's predictions.

## 2.6. Intra-Industry Trade:

The traditional models of trade were set out by the model of David Ricardo and the Heckscher-Ohlin model which tried to explain the occurrence of international trade. Both models used the idea of comparative advantage and an explanation of why countries trade. However, many economists have made the point of claiming that these models provide no explanation towards intra-industry trade as under their assumptions countries with identical factor endowments would not trade and produce goods domestically. Hence, over the past three decades as intra-industry trade has developed many economists have looked at other explanations.

### 2.5.6 Meaning of Intra Industry Trade :

Intra-industry trade refers to the exchange of products belonging to the same industry. The term is usually applied to international trade where the same kinds of goods and services are both imported and exported. Examples of this kind of trade include automobiles, foodstuffs and beverages, computers and minerals. Intra-industry trade represents international trade within industries rather than between industries. Such trade is more beneficial than inter-industry trade because it stimulates innovation and exploits economies of scale. Moreover, since productive factors do not switch from one industry to another but only within industries, intra-industry trade is less disruptive than inter-industry trade.

### 2.5.7 Significance of Intra Industry Trade :

Significance of Intra-Industry Trade can explain with the help of following points:

1) **Need not be based on Competitive Advantages :**

   The significance of intra-industry trade arises from its basic character. It need not be based on comparative advantage. To a large extent, intra-industry trade arises from the facts that products are differentiated and the production of any particular product requires some fixed costs. Thus, the more sport utility vehicles Ford makes the lower the unit cost; the more Mercedes-Benz convertibles produced, the lower the unit cost. Some elements of comparative advantage may be involved; for example, Germany may have a comparative advantage in producing high-quality cars. However, the automobile industry is now a world industry. To the extent that comparative advantage is not involved, the pattern of trade is indeterminate. When economies of scale are involved who exports what can be determined by accident of history.

2) **Need Not Cause Dislocations :**

   One of the great benefits of intra-industry trade is that international trade need not cause the dislocations associated with inter-industry trade. The Stolper-Samuelson theorem suggests that international trade can cause a redistribution of income from scarce factors to abundant factors. But if most international trade is intra-industry, the impact on internal income distribution should be relatively minor. If trade is not based on scarce and abundant factors of production, it does not result in reduced demand for the scarce factors and increased demand for the abundant factors; thus, trade expansion need not result in large changes in the distribution of income.

3) **Enhances Gains :**

Intra-industry trade enhances the gains from trade through better exploitation of economies of scale rather than through comparative advantage as trade leads countries to concentrate on a limited number of products within any particular industry. This leads to an expansion of world output because of the saving of fixed costs.

4) **Innovation :**

Specialisation within industrial categories may also stimulate innovation. Producing a greater variety and number of goods increases our general knowledge about technology and greater knowledge implies smaller costs of knowledge accumulation. For example, U.S. importation of Japanese cars and trucks has led to improvements in U.S. car and truck manufacturers.

5) **Reduction in Demand for Protection :**

Intra-industry trade reduces the demands for protection because in any industry, there are both exports and imports, making it difficult to achieve unanimity among those demanding protection. Intra-industry trade need not give rise to a justification for a strategic trade policy that is, giving export subsidies to correct for departures from perfect competition. It is true that much intra-industry trade takes place under imperfect competition but monopolistic competition is for all practical purposes efficient.

❖❖❖❖❖❖❖❖❖

## Review Questions

**Q. 1. Answer in 100 Words:**

1) State the Origin and Background of Absolute Cost Advantages.
2) Explain the Meaning ad Origin of Comparative Cost Advantages.
3) State the Determinants of Comparative Cost Advantages.
4) Explain the Criticisms of Heckscher-Ohlin Theory.
5) State the Limitations of the Rybczynski Theorem.

**Q. 2. Answer in 200 Words:**

1) Critically Examine the Theory of Absolute Cost Advantages.
2) Discuss the Criticisms of Theory of Comparative Cost Advantages.
3) Explain the Assumptions of Heckscher-Ohlin Theory.
4) Discuss the Importance of Intra-Industry Trade.
5) Write in detail about the Leontief Paradox.

**Q. 3. Answer in 400 Words:**

1) Explain the Theory of Absolute Cost Advantages.
2) Discuss in detail about the Theory of Comparative Cost Advantages.
3) Explain in detail Heckscher-Ohlin Theory.
4) What is Intra-Industry Trade? Explain its Importance.
5) Discuss in detail about the Rybczynski Theorem.

**Q. 4. Answer in 20 Words:**

1) Absolute Cost Advantages.
2) Comparative Cost Advantages.
3) Heckscher-Ohlin Theory.
4) Leontief Paradox.
5) Intra-Industry Trade.
6) Rybczynski Theorem.

❖❖❖❖❖❖❖❖

# Gain from Trade

**UNIT 3**



## Introduction:

The concept of Terms of Trade is one of the most significant concepts used in the theory of international economics. It is a quantitative measure of the rate at which a country's exports and imports are exchanged against each other. The terms of trade receive considerable attention in the discussion of international economic problems at least for two reasons (i) the from trade depend upon the terms of trade, (ii) the Third World countries feel that their products have suffered a secular deterioration in their terms of trade as a result of which there has been an unjust transfer of income from the poor to the rich countries who have improved their terms of trade at the expense of the poor countries. The very basis of international trade is that it is mutually advantageous to all the If India imports cars, radios, machinery and other technical equipment from England and England imports raw jute and tea from India, it means that in the absence of international trade these countries would either have been deprived of these goods or would have incurred higher costs if they produced these goods themselves. In either case, both the countries would have been losers. The gain from trade, therefore, is that (i) the different countries can obtain goods which they themselves cannot produce and can thereby improve the standard of living of the people, and (ii) they can obtain these goods at much cheaper prices than would have been possible if they produced the goods themselves.

## 3.1 Gains from Trade:

Gains from Trade can be traced to Ricardian Theory where it was stated that international trade leads to increase in the sum of enjoyments. In modern terms we say that International Trade is a positive sum game. These gains are measured by increase in real income of participating countries.

### 3.1.1 Meaning:

According to mercantilist and classical economists, international trade makes international division of labour and specialization possible. As a result of it, all countries of the world stand to gain. On account of international trade based on the principle of comparative costs and consequent specialization and division of labour, the gain that the trading countries enjoy is called gain from international trade. Thus, gain from international trade refers to that advantage which different countries participating in international trade, enjoy as a result of specialization and division of labour. As a consequence of these gains, different countries make optimum use of their resources and thus maximize their production, extend the size of market and increase their national income.

### 3.1.2 Definitions:

The following are the definitions of gain from trade:

1) **Paul Samuelson:**
*"Gain from trade refers to the overall increase in economic welfare that arises from specialization and exchange between countries. It is the net benefit that each country can achieve by focusing on producing and exporting goods or services in which it has a comparative advantage."*

2) **Adam Smith:**
*"The gain from trade is the increase in total output and consumption that can be achieved when countries specialize in producing goods or services in which they have a comparative advantage and engage in voluntary trade with one another. Through trade, countries can expand their consumption possibilities beyond what they can produce domestically."*

3) **David Ricardo:**
*"The gain from trade results from the principle of comparative advantage, where countries specialize in producing goods or services in which they have a lower opportunity cost compared to other countries. By trading with each other, countries can consume more of all goods involved in trade, leading to mutual gains."*

4) **Jagdish Bhagwati:**
*"Gain from trade refers to the welfare improvement that arises from trade liberalization and the removal of barriers to international trade. It includes the benefits of increased consumer choices, lower prices, technological spillovers, and economies of scale that result from engaging in international trade."*

### 3.1.3 Sources of Gains:

Main sources of gains from trade as under:

1) **Division of Labour:**

   It is clear from Richardo's theory of comparative costs that when different countries of the world specialize in the production of those goods in which enjoy greater comparative advantage or they have least comparative disadvantage, then all the trading countries will stand to gain. Thus one of the main sources of gain from trade is division of labour on the basis of comparative costs.

2) **International Specialisation:**

   Another main source of gain from international trade is specialization based on the comparative cost advantage. It makes possible large-scale production, which in its turn, yields internal and external economics. These economies give rise to gains from trade.

3) **Wide Extent of Market:**

   Scale of production increases as a result of wide extent of the market. Scope of division of labour and specialization widens. Consequently, cost of production falls and so also that price of the commodity. It also constitutes gain from the international trade.

### 3.1.4 Kinds of Gain:

The gains from trade are divided into static and dynamic gains which are discussed as under:

A) **Static Gains:**

   The following are the static gains from trade:

1) **Maximisation of Production:**

   According to the classical economists, the gains from trade result from the advantages of division of labour and specialisation both at the national and international levels. Given the resources and technology in a country, it is specialisation in production on the basis of comparative advantage and trading which enables each country to exchange its goods for the goods of another country. Thus, it reaps greater gain than without trade. Each country exports those goods which it produces cheaper in exchange for what other countries produce at a lower cost. According to Ricardo, "The gain from trade consisted in the saving of cost resulting from obtaining the imported goods through trade instead of domestic production." Thus, trade maximises production.

2) **Increase in Welfare:**

   As a result of international division of labour and specialisation, the production of goods increases in the trading country. As a result, the consumption of goods increases and so does the welfare of the people. As pointed out by Ricardo, "The extension of international trade very powerfully contributes to increase the mass of commodities and, therefore, the sum of enjoyments."

3) **Increase in National Income:**

When a country gains from international specialisation and exchange of goods in trade, there is increase in its national income. This, in turn, raises its level of output and growth rate of the economy.

4) **Vent for Surplus:**

The gain from trade also arises from the existence of idle land, labour, and other resources in a country before it enters into international trade. With its opening (vent) to world markets, its resources are used to produce a surplus of goods which would otherwise remain unsold. This is Adam Smith's vent for surplus gain from trade.

B) **Dynamic Gains:**

The following are the dynamic gains from trade:

1) **Efficient Employment of Resources:**

The direct dynamic gains from foreign trade are that comparative advantage leads to a more efficient employment of the productive resources of the world.

2) **Widens-the Market:**

The major indirect dynamic gain from trade is that it widens the size of the market. By enlarging the size of the market and scope of specialisation, international trade makes a greater use of machines, encourages inventions and innovations, raises labour productivity, lowers costs and leads to faster growth.

3) **Development of Other Activities:**

When a country starts producing goods for export and importing goods for domestic consumption, other economic activities also develop. There is expansion of infrastructure facilities in power, and building highways, bridges, fly-overs etc. Shopping and housing complexes are built along with industrial centres. The primary sector develops into business sector for export of raw materials and for domestic use. Tertiary sector expands in the form of banks, communications, insurance etc.

4) **Increase in Investments:**

Foreign trade encourages the setting up of new units for assembling and production of variety of goods. Supplementary and ancillary units are established. Production for exports leads to backward and forward linkages in developing other activities referred to above. All these increase autonomous and induced investments in the country.

## 3.2 Terms of Trade:

The concept of terms of trade is one of the most significant concepts used in the theory of international economics. It is a quantitative measure of the rate at which a country's exports and imports are exchanged against each other. The terms of trade receive considerable attention in the discussion of international economic problems at least for two reasons (i) the gains from trade depend upon the terms of trade, (ii) the third world countries feel that their products have suffered a secular deterioration in their terms of trade as a result of which there has been an unjust transfer of income from the poor to the rich countries who have improved their terms of trade at the expense of the poor countries. In international trade, terms of trade is most widely used concept by the policy maker because it is relatively easy to understand and convenient to explain the country's balance of payments difficulties. There is similarity of technicalities of terms of trade for both the developed and developing economies, due to the greater sensitivity of prices of raw material over the business cycle of the developed economies, the greater dependence of the developing economies on fewer export goods and pivotal role of international trade in promoting economic growth.

### 3.2.1 Meaning :

The terms of trade refer to the rate at which the goods of one country exchange for the goods of another country. It is a measure of the purchasing power of exports of a country in terms of its imports and is expressed as the relation between export prices and import prices of its goods. When the export prices of a country raise, relatively to its import prices, its terms of trade are said to have improved. On the other hand, when its import prices raise relatively to its export prices, its terms of trade are said to have worsened. The country's gain from trade is reduced because it can have a smaller quantity of imports in exchange for a given quantity of exports than before.

### 3.2.2 Definitions :

Here are a few definitions of "Terms of Trade" provided by notable authors:

1) **Paul Samuelson:**
   "Terms of trade refer to the ratio at which a country can exchange its exports for imports. It represents the purchasing power of a country's exports in relation to its imports and indicates the relative prices of exports and imports in international trade."
2) **Joseph Stiglitz:**
   "Terms of trade represent the ratio of the price of a country's exports to the price of its imports. It reflects the terms on which a country participates in international trade, indicating the relative value of its exports compared to its imports."
3) **Jagdish Bhagwati:**
   "Terms of trade refer to the rate at which a country can exchange its exports for imports. It measures the amount of imports a country can obtain in exchange for a given quantity of its exports and reflects the economic conditions of international trade for that country."

4) **Milton Friedman:**
"Terms of trade represent the ratio of export prices to import prices. It indicates the terms at which a country can trade its goods and services in the international market and reflects the relative value of what a country exports compared to what it imports."

## 3.2.3 Importance of Terms of Trade :

Terms of trade are vital importance in determining the gains in which a country obtains from international trade. These terms of trade not only have a bearing on the quantum of international trade but also the quality of trade between the nations. As the international trade is a continuous relationship between countries and they also define the direction of a country's external relations as well. The significance or the importance of terms of trade can be explained as follows:

1) **Economic Welfare and Terms of Trade :**
A country's terms of trade has a significant bearing on the welfare of the economy as no country in the contemporary world can remain in isolation and it is forced to trade with other countries. However, it should be ensured that the terms of trade negotiated are to the maximum benefit of the economy. Economic growth achieved within the country through expansion in real production and productivity through efficiency will fail to increase welfare and living standards in the country at terms of trade constantly deteriorate. That is, if the commodity terms of trade which is an indicator of gains from trade are adverse then it would cause an immiserising effect on the economy.

2) **Terms of Trade and Balance of Payment :**
Terms of trade and the balance of payment situation of any country is inextricably inter related as the effect of terms of trade is an important component of the total balance of payments situation. If the terms of trade are adverse, it will also adversely affect the balance of payment situation.

3) **Terms of Trade and the Volume of International Trade :**
Terms of trade in terms of net barter or commodity terms of trade has an important bearing on the volume of trade and the cumulative effect of the commodity terms and price terms determine the net improvement in the economic welfare of the country due to international trade. The commodity terms of trade and the price terms of trade have amongst themselves a complementary effect on each other in determining the complexion of the trade between the countries.

4) **Terms of Trade - Factorial Terms of Trade :**
Terms of trade which is understood synonymously with the commodity terms of trade has a bearing on the factorial terms of trade as well as the mobility of factors of

production. Be it material labour, capital or organisation from countries where they are in abundance to countries, where they are scarce and there is greater demand in consonance with the factor prices between countries. As the economies get integrated due to growing international trade even the labour tends to move fast and far from the places where the wages are low to economies which are ready to pay more.

5) **International Economic Growth - a Product of Reasonable Terms of Trade :** Reasonable and scientifically developed terms of trade which are sensitive to the ground realities of international trade would bring in equilibrium in the international economy as a whole and the growing wealth and incomes of the world are equitably redistributed having regard to the area, population and the gross productive potential of the countries.

### 3.2.4 Types of Terms of Trade :

There are various types of terms of trade. These are the income terms of trade, the single factoral terms of trade and the double factoral terms of trade. The commodity, or net barter, terms of trade (N) is the ratio of the price index of the country's exports (Px), to the price index of its imports (Pm), multiplied by 100 (to express the terms of trade in percentages).

A) **Gross Barter Terms of Trade:**

According to Prof. Taussig, Gross Barter Terms of Trade refer to the total quantities of exports and imports of a country exchanged for each other at a particular point of time or in a particular year as compared to some selected base year's total exports and total imports of that country.

The distinction between "gross" and "net" barter terms of trade was introduced by Taussig in 1927. Symbolically, we can express gross barter terms as follows:

Here,

Mq = Stands for the import quantity index.

Xq = Stands for export quantity index.

G = Stands for gross barter term.

The whole expression is multiplied by 100 in order to get rid of the decimal. It is to be noted that there is no other significance to this number.

**Example:**

The concept can be explained more clearly with some concrete examples as follows:

The quantity index of imports and exports for the base year (say 2012) will always be equal to 100. The base year will serve as the benchmark period with which the changes in the gross barter terms of trade in any given subsequent year can be measured say 2013, 2014, 2020 etc. Look at the following hypothetical sets:

$$2012 \text{ Based Year } G = \frac{100}{100} \times 100 = 100 \text{ (Based year)}$$

$$2013 \quad G = \frac{120}{100} \times 100 = 100 \text{ (Improvement)}$$

$$2014 \quad G = \frac{120}{120} \times 100 = 100 \text{ (No Change)}$$

$$2016 \quad G = \frac{100}{120} \times 100 = 83.33 \text{ (Deterionation)}$$

For 2013, the import quantity index is up from 100 to 120 and the export quantity is the same. This means that in 2013, the export quantity is same as in 2012 but import is more in 2013 than in 2012. In other words, the purchasing power of exports has gone up in 2013 compared to the base year 2012. There has been, therefore, a 20% point improvement in the gross barter terms of trade in 2013 as compared to the year 2012. In 2014, compared with the base year 2012, however, there has been no change in gross barter terms because both the import and export quantity index numbers have gone up from 100 to 120 between these two periods. The gross barter terms of trade index are 100 both for 2012 and 2014. In 2015, as compared to base year 2012, there has been deterioration in gross barter terms. The import quantity index is constant at 100 both for 2015 and the base year 2012 but the export quantity index for 2015 is 120 as against the base period index of 100. This means that in 2015, the import quantity is same as in 2014 but paying more for these imports as indicated by the increase in the export quantity index (From 120 in 2012 to 120 in 2015). In brief, an increase in the import quantity index tends to improve gross barter terms while an increase in the export quantity index would tend to worsen the gross barter terms of trade. This concept has its own merits but it is not commonly used expression of the terms of trade concept in today's world. The concept of gross barter terms of trade was considered better than the concept of net barter terms of trade. But there are certain deficiencies in it that resulted in its criticism.

1) **Aggregation of Goods, Services and Capital Transactions:**

The gross barter terms of trade attempted to remove the deficiency of the net barter terms of trade by aggregating all exports of goods, services and capital in the index of export quantities. Similarly, the imports of goods, services and capital were aggregated in the index of quantities imported. The lumping together of these non-homogeneous quantities was both unreal and impractical. It was because of this reason that this concept of terms of trade came to be rejected at the hands of economists like Jacob Viner and Haberler.

**2) Faulty Index of Welfare:**

A higher ratio of quantity index of imports to the quantity index of exports is sometimes regarded as an index of a higher level of welfare from trade because the country obtains larger quantity of importable good per unit of exportable goods. But this is not necessarily true. If there are such changes in tastes and habits of a people that even a smaller quantity of imports yields greater satisfaction, the community may derive greater welfare despite unfavourable gross barter terms of trade.

**3) Neglect of Productivity:**

It is possible that a country has unfavourable gross barter terms of trade but that is caused by increased factor productivity in the export sector. The increased factor productivity still indicates the gain from the point of view of the exporting country. The impact of improvement in productivity has been overlooked in this measure of terms of trade.

**4) Neglect of Qualitative Changes:**

The gross barter terms of trade ratio undoubtedly takes into account the physical quantities of imports and exports but ignores the fact that there might have been qualitative improvements in production in the exporting and importing countries. Such changes can have very significant effect on the welfare, yet these are not reflected through the gross barter terms of trade.

**5) Neglect of Capital Movements:**

The international capital movements have quite important influence on the balance of payments and general economic condition of a country. This vital factor, however, has not found proper expression in the measurement of gross barter terms of trade.

**B) Net Barter Terms of Trade:**

The use of commodity terms of trade has been accepted as the most useful device in order to measure the short term changes in the trading position of a country. The application of the commodity terms of trade is so popular and general that whenever we talk of the terms of trade, we mean the commodity terms of trade.

**1) Meaning of Net Barter Terms of Trade :**

Net barter terms of trade refer to the ratio of export prices to import prices at a given period of time compared to an earlier year selected as the base year. The gross barter terms concept uses quantity index for imports and exports whereas the net barter or commodity terms concept makes use of the price index for imports and exports.

Symbolically the Net Barter Terms of Trade can be written as follows:

$$N = \frac{X_p}{M_p} \times 100$$

Here,

Xp = Stands for exports price index numbers.

Mp = Stands for price index numbers of imports.

N = Stands for net barter or commodity terms.

As in the previous case, the expression is multiplied by 100 only to get rid of the decimal.

**2) Example of Net Barter Terms of Trade :**

The price index of the imports and exports for the base year (say 2000) will always be 100. The commodity terms changes in the subsequent year are expressed with reference to the base year index. Look at the following hypothetical set of commodity price index numbers of imports and exports.

**3) Commodity Terms of Trade Index :**

$$2010\text{(Based Year) } N = \frac{100}{100} \times 100 = 100 \text{ (Based Year)}$$

$$2011 \qquad N = \frac{120}{100} = 100 = 120 \text{ (Improvement)}$$

$$2012 \qquad N = \frac{100}{120} = 100 = 83.33 \text{ (Detesteralion)}$$

$$2013 \qquad N = \frac{120}{120} \times 100 = 100 \text{ (No Charge)}$$

$$2014 \qquad N = \frac{85}{80} \times 100 = 120 \text{ (Based Year)}$$

$$2016 \qquad N = \frac{126}{140} = 100 = 90 \text{ (Deberiandtion)}$$

**4) Explanation of Net barter terms of trade :**

In 2011, there is an improvement in commodity terms by 20% points because we buy our imports at the same price as in 2010 but sell our exports at a higher price. In 2012, there is deterioration in commodity terms because we sell our exports at the same price as in 2010 but buy our imports at a higher price. In 2013, however, there has been an increase in both the export and import price index by the same percentage point i.e. 20% which leaves the terms of trade unchanged. In 2014, there has been a decrease in both import and export price index and in 2015, there has been an increase in both index numbers in such a way that commodity terms have turned favourable in 2014 but unfavourable in 2015 as compared to the base year 2010.

**5) Rule of Net Barter Terms of Trade :**

The simple rule is that if there is an increase in our selling price (export price index), there will be an improvement in commodity terms and if there is an increase in our buying price (import price index), there will be an unfavourable movement in commodity terms of trade.

**6) Criticisms:**

Even though the concept of net barter terms of trade has been widely accepted as a useful measure of short-term changes in the trade position of a country, yet it suffers from certain limitations because of which it has been subjected to criticism. The main objections against it are as follows:

**a) Problems in the Construction of Index Numbers:**

This concept involves the use of index numbers of export and import prices. The construction of index numbers is beset with several problems related to the choice of commodities, obtaining of price quotations, choice of base year, use of appropriate weights and the method for computing index numbers.

**b) Neglect of Qualitative Changes:**

The net barter terms of trade are based on indices of export and import prices. These can measure the relative changes in prices between the current and base period. If there are qualitative changes in output in the two trading countries during a given period, they remain neglected. In such a situation, net barter terms of trade cannot measured exactly the changes in welfare due to foreign trade in general and terms of trade in particular.

**c) Misleading:**

If the export price index of a country falls, the import price index remaining the same, there is worsening of the net barter terms of trade. As export prices are lower than the import prices, the country will be able to get a smaller quantity of import in exchange of the goods exported. The conclusion may be derived that the economic position of the country has deteriorated. It is possible that the fall in export prices has resulted from a fall in costs of producing export goods.

If the productivity in export sector increases at a greater rate than the worsening of net barter terms of trade, the country actually does not suffer due to trade, it rather gains. From this it follows that the net barter terms of trade can sometimes result in misleading conclusions.

**d) Inappropriate for Explaining Distribution of Gains from Trade:**

The concept of net barter terms of trade is an inappropriate criterion for explaining the distribution of gains from trade between two countries one of which is advanced and the other is less developed. Suppose the import price index has risen relatively less than the export price index in the latter. It signifies an improvement in the terms of trade and the conclusion is derived that the less developed country gains from trade.

However, if the profits from foreign investments rise large enough to off-set the increase in export prices, the LDC may not derive any gain from trade. Similarly, if the export prices fall but there is also an equivalent fall in the profits of foreign investments, the position of the country is not worse off even though the net barter terms of trade are unfavourable. It is, therefore, evident that the distribution of gains from trade cannot be rightly decided on the basis of changes just in the net barter terms of trade.

e) **Faulty Index of Gain from Trade:**

It is often claimed that the net barter terms of trade provide an index of gains from trade for a country. In this connection, Taussig pointed out that the net barter terms of trade could be an appropriate measure of gains from trade, if the balance of payments of the country included only the receipts and payments on account of exchange of goods and services. However, if balance of payments includes also the capital transactions and unilateral transfers, the gain from trade cannot be determined through the ratio of export and import prices.

f) **Period of Time:**

The net barter terms of trade are based upon the relative changes in export and import prices over some period between the base year and the current year. If this time interval is too short, there may not be any significant change in the terms of trade. On the contrary, if this duration is too long, there is the possibility of some major changes in the structure of production and demand in the countries such that comparisons on the basis of export and import prices are rendered irrelevant.

g) **Neglect of Factors Affecting Prices:**

The net barter terms of trade concentrate only upon the indices of export and import prices. There is absolute neglect of the factors, which cause variation in these prices. The export and import prices are affected by changes in productivity, costs, wages, general business conditions and reciprocal demand in the trading countries. Any conclusion concerning the economic position of a country exclusively on the basis of commodity terms of trade cannot be valid.

h) **Capacity to Import:**

The improvement or worsening of the commodity terms of trade cannot give any definite conclusion about the capacity of a country to import. An appropriate measure of the capacity to import can be the income terms of trade rather than the net barter terms of trade. In order to overcome the deficiencies of the net barter terms of trade, Taussig introduced the concept of gross barter terms of trade.

C) **Income Terms of Trade:**

The concept of the income terms of trade is of great relevance in the context of the underdeveloped countries whose capacity to import is very low. The concept of income terms of trade was first formulated by G.S. Dorrance in 1948-49. This term takes into account the volume of exports of a country and its export prices and import prices. This concept shows a country's changing import capacity in relation to changes in its exports. Thus, the income terms of trade index is the net barter term of trade of a country multiplied by its export volume index? Symbolically, it can be written as follows:

$$I = NX_q \left( \alpha I = \frac{X_P}{M_P} \times X_q \;\; \alpha I = \frac{X_p X_q}{M_D} \right)$$

Here,

N = Refers to net barter or commodity terms of trade index.

Xq = Stands for the export quantity index.

I = Stands for income terms of trade.

Mp = Stands for price index numbers of imports.

Xp = Stands for exports price index numbers.

Look at the following sets of cases:

Income Terms of Trade Index:

$$2013 \qquad I = \frac{100 \times 100}{100} = 100 \text{ (Based Year)}$$

$$2014 \qquad I = \frac{90 \times 120}{100} = 108 \text{ (Improvement)}$$

$$2016 \qquad I = \frac{110 \times 90}{100} = 98 \text{ (Deterloration)}$$

An income term of trade index is 100 for the base year 2013. Now, in 2014, there has been a fall in the export price index with no change in the import price index suggesting that commodity terms have worsened. But there has been an increase in the export quantity index from 100 to 120 in 2014. A 10 percentage point decrease in the export price index is, therefore, matched by a 20 percentage point increase in the export quantity index so that in the end there has been 8 percentage point improvement in the terms of trade in 2014 compared with the base year 2013. In other words, between 2013 and 2014, income terms of trade have improved although the commodity terms of trade have worsened and the country is better off as reflected by the changes in income terms of trade. In 2015, as compared with 2013, however, the situation is opposite. Commodity terms have improved by 10 percentage points but income terms have deteriorated by 12 percentage points. Income terms of trade have worsened in 2015 even though the commodity terms have improved in that year. The country has been worse off in 2015 as compared to 2013 due to the worsening of income terms of trade. The concept of income terms of trade is criticised on the following grounds:

1) **Not an Accurate Measure of Gain from Trade:**

This concept cannot give an exact measure of the gain from trade. An improvement in income terms of trade may show that the capacity of a country to import has increased. It will force the country to raise its exports large enough to pay for imports. If the increased exports involve some depletion of real resources of the country, the long run growth potential and prospect of improving the standard of living are adversely affected.

2) **Not a Measure of Total Import Capacity:**

The income terms of trade measure only the export- based import capacity of a country and not its total import capacity which depends also upon its foreign exchange receipts. It is possible that income terms of trade of a country get worsened but the foreign exchange reserves have risen for some reasons that will mean a larger total import capacity despite adverse income terms of trade.

3) **Cannot Replace the Commodity Terms of Trade:**

It is sometimes believed that the income terms of trade are superior to the commodity terms of trade. In view of contradictory conclusions given by the two indices, the former alone is clearly inadequate. It can supplement but by no means replace the commodity terms of trade or net barter terms of trade.

4) **Misleading Indicator of Welfare Gain:**

The income terms of trade may prove to be a faulty and misleading indicator of direction of change of the welfare of a country. From this point of view, the net barter terms of trade can serve as a better indicator of welfare gain to a country from the international trade.

D) **Single Factoral Terms of Trade:**

The concept of commodity terms of trade does not take account of productivity changes in export industries. Professor Viner has developed the concept of single factoral terms of trade which allows changes in the domestic export sector. It is calculated by multiplying the commodity terms of trade index by an index of productivity changes in domestic export industries. It can be expressed as:

$$Ts = Tc.Fx = \frac{Px.Fx}{Pm}$$

Where:

Ts = the single factoral terms of trade,

Tc = the commodity terms of trade, and

Rx = the productivity index of export industries.

It shows that a country's factoral terms of trade improve as productivity improves in its export industries. If the productivity of a country's exports industries increases, its factoral terms of trade may improve even though its commodity terms of trade may deteriorate.

**For Example:**

The prices of its exports may all relatively to its import prices as a result of increase in the productivity of the export industries of a country. The commodity terms of trade will deteriorate but its factoral terms of trade will show an improvement.

**Criticisms:**

This measure of terms of trade is, however, criticised on the following main grounds:

1) **Difficulty in the Measurement of Productivity:**

The exact measurement of productivity and changes therein is quite difficult, as factor productivity depends upon some non-quantifiable psychological and technical factors. The productivity of a factor unit differs not only from one export industry to another but also from one plant to another. That causes serious complication in the computation of productivity index and changes in it over different periods.

2) **Not a Reliable Index of Gain from Trade:**

The terms of trade are supposed to be an index of gains from international trade of a country. It is possible that increase in productivity index makes the single factoral terms of trade favourable but the rise in productivity in export sector and consequent fall in production costs and export price index can transfer the gain from higher productivity and trade to the foreign country. The productivity increase may occur in the exporting country but the productivity and trade gains go to the importing country.

3) **Increase in Global Inequalities:**

The increased productivity in the export sectors of the advanced countries like U.S.A., Japan and the West European countries has brought about considerable improvement in their single factoral terms of trade while keeping their net barter terms of trade also favourable for them. However, the improvement in productivity in the export sectors in the LDC's has made both commodity terms of trade and single factoral terms of trade unfavourable. This has happened because the export prices of poor countries have been secularly declining, whereas the export prices of advanced countries have remained higher despite a rise in productivity. This has accentuated the global inequalities of income and wealth. For this crucial reason, the single factoral terms of trade cannot be an appropriate index of welfare and living standards.

4) **Neglect of Increase in Productivity in Foreign Countries:**

The single factoral terms of trade give importance only to improvement in the productivity in the export sector. It fails to take into account the possible change in the productivity in the foreign countries and their resultant effect on the terms of trade. This deficiency was removed by Jacob Viner through his introduction of the concept of double factoral terms of trade.

E) **Double Factoral Terms of Trade:**

The double factoral terms of trade take into account productivity change both in the domestic export sector and the foreign export sector producing the country's imports. The index measuring the double factoral terms of trade can be expressed.

$$Td = \frac{TC.Fx}{Fm} = \frac{Px.Fx}{Pm.Fm}$$

$$Tc = \frac{Px}{Pm}$$

Where:

Td = the double factoral terms of trade,

Px/Pm = the commodity terms of trade

Fx = the import productivity index and Fm is the import productivity index.

**1) Advantages of Double Factoral Terms of Trade :**

It helps in measuring the change in the rate of exchange of a country as a result of the change in the productive efficiency of domestic factors manufacturing exports and that of foreign factors manufacturing imports for that country. A rise in the index of double factoral terms of trade of a country means that the productive efficiency of the factors producing exports has increased relatively to the factors producing imports in the other country.

**2) Criticisms:**

The concept of double factoral terms of trade has met with criticism on the following main grounds:

**a) Measurement of Productivity:**

Like single factoral terms of trade, this concept too has a limitation related to exact measurement of productivity of the factors and changes therein both in the export sectors of home country and the foreign country. Although E. Devons attempted to compute single factoral terms of trade in Britain for 1948-53 periods, yet no significant headway could be made in the computation of double factoral terms of trade.

**b) Misplaced Emphasis:**

The double factoral terms of trade emphasises upon the relative productivity indices in the two trading countries. Such an emphasis seems to be misplaced. The matter which is of greater concern for any country is the quantities of commodities that can be imported with a given quantity of its exports rather than the quantity of productive factors required in a foreign country to produce the goods imported by the home country. This line of argument suggests that even gross barter terms of trade are better than the double factoral terms of trade.

**c) Faulty Concept:**

This concept attempts to establish a relation between the productivity of the factors in two trading countries. Kindleberger has objected to it and has regarded this concept as faulty. He even treats single factoral terms of trade as a better concept than the double factoral terms of trade. In his words, "The single factoral term of trade is a much more relevant concept than the double factoral terms of trade. We are interested in what our factors can earn in goods, not what our factor services can command in services of foreign factor."

d) **Difficulty in the Determination of Gains from Trade:**

It is difficult to measure the gains from trade for a country with the help of this concept of terms of trade. The relative changes in factor productivity in two trading countries can affect the quantities of exported and imported goods and their respective prices in such a way that the conclusion about the gains from trade cannot be easily derived.

e) **Neglect of Real Costs:**

When the two trading countries make efforts to increase the production of export goods, there is diversion of productive resources including some additional real cost. The concept ignores the real cost as a factor influencing the terms as well as the gains from trade. This deficiency was, however, removed through the concept of real cost terms of trade.

### 3.2.5 Determinants of Terms of Trade :

An improvement of a nation's terms of trade benefits that country in the sense that it can buy more imports for any given level of exports. The terms of trade may be influenced by the exchange rate because a rise in the value of a country's currency lowers the domestic prices of its imports but may not directly affect the prices of the commodities it exports. Following are the factors which effects on term of trade.

1) **Reciprocal Demand :**

Terms of trade (TOT) will depend upon the demand of each country for the other country's product. Suppose there are two countries England and Portugal. England produces cloth and Portugal produces wine. If the demand of England for wine is inelastic (i.e. if price - the demand does not change) and the demand for cloth of Portugal is elastic (i.e. the price of cloth, the demand for cloth also changes then the TOT will be in favour of Portugal. An increase in price of wine does not affect the England's demand for wine. If the TOT moves in favour of Portugal then the TOT will be against England. Each country's demand for other country's product affects the TOT. Actual TOT will depend upon the elasticity of demand.

2) **Changes in Factor Endowments :**

Changes in the factor endowments affect terms of trade. Factor endowments mean the availability of factors of production in a country. This affects the volume of production and thereby the prices of export and import goods, changes in factor endowments may increase exports or reduce them. If the tastes and habits of country remain unchanged, this will lead to changes in TOT. If the factors of production in country 'A' increases then the country 'A' will produce more commodities and try to export more. But if there is no change in the factors of production of country 'B', the country 'B' will not increase in production. Here the TOT will move in favour of country 'B' and against 'A'.

3) **Change in Technology :**

Technological change also affects the TOT of a country. Suppose, before technological change, Portugal exports wine and imports cloth from England. After the technological change, if Portugal likes to export less wine and imports less of cloth than England and wants to exchange at the previous TOT, the TOT of Portugal improves. Portugal is better because it exports less wine for more of England's cloth. So, Portugal's TOT has improved with technological change.

4) **Changes in Taste :**

Changes in taste of the people of a country also influence terms of trade with another country. Suppose England's taste shifts from Germany's linen to its own cloth, the terms of trade of England will improve. England will export less of cloth to Germany and its demand for Germany's linen will fall.

5) **Economic Growth :**

Economic growth is another important factor which affects the terms of trade. The raising of a country's national product or income over a time is called economic growth. An increase in the productive capacity may affect favourably or adversely its terms of trade. Suppose, there is a trade between England and Germany, before growth the terms of trade are determined by some ratio. It's Germany before growth the terms of trade are determined by some ratio. If new growth takes place in England then the production possibility curve of England shifts and new TOT would be in favour of England.

6) **Tariff:**

An import tariff improves TOT of the imposing country. Suppose, there are a trade between England and Germany, England imposes tariff on Germany's goods. Then the volume of imports reduces and thereby the TOT would be definitely in favour of England.

7) **Devaluation :**

On account of devaluation, the external value of home currency declines. Devaluation means reducing the value of home currency in relation with the foreign currency. RBI devalues the home currency. It is a measure to correct the adverse balance of payment. The effect of devaluation is to increase the exports and decrease the imports. The terms of trade are improved. But the success of devaluation depends upon the elasticity's of demand for the goods. Devaluation leads to the increase in the prices of imports and fall in the prices of exports.

8) **Capital Inflows and Outflows :**

When a country borrows from abroad, it results in an increase in demand for goods of creditor countries and pushes up their prices. This results in influencing the terms of trade. In the same way, when the time for the repayment of the loan comes, the required foreign currencies must be obtained any how to pay the loan back to the creditor country. This may require selling domestically produced goods rather cheaply to get the required hard currency. This may result in making terms of trade less favourable for the debtor country.

**9) Balance of Payments :**

If a country has been facing continuously adverse balance of trade and payments, the country will have either to devalue its currency or follow the policy of deflation to correct the adverse balance of trade and payments position. This would make the terms of trade go against the country facing continuously adverse balance of trade and payments.

## 3.3 Reciprocal Demand and Derivation of Offer Curves:

Reciprocal demand refers to the relationship between the quantities of goods that two countries are willing to import from each other at different relative prices. It is a fundamental concept in international trade analysis that helps us understand the determinants of trade patterns and the benefits of international trade. The reciprocal demand between two countries is influenced by factors such as relative prices, incomes, tastes, and trade policies. To analyze reciprocal demand and its implications, economists use offer curves. Offer curves depict the quantities of goods a country is willing to export at different world prices, taking into account the relative prices of goods within the country. Offer curves are derived based on the assumptions of perfect competition, constant costs, and fixed resources. In this essay, we will explore the concept of reciprocal demand, discuss the derivation of offer curves, and highlight the key insights they provide in the field of international trade.

### 3.3.1 Reciprocal Demand :

Reciprocal demand is a concept that examines the relationship between the quantities of goods that two countries are willing to import from each other at different relative prices. It is a reflection of the demand for a country's exports in terms of the other country's imports. The reciprocal demand curve shows the quantities of goods that a country will import from another country at various relative prices. It is derived by combining the import demand curves of both countries.

To understand reciprocal demand, we need to examine the factors that influence it. First, relative prices play a crucial role. If the relative price of a good in one country decreases compared to another country, it becomes relatively cheaper and more attractive for importation. This leads to an increase in the reciprocal demand for that good. On the other hand, if the relative price of good increases, its reciprocal demand decreases.

Second, income levels impact reciprocal demand. As incomes rise, consumers tend to demand more goods, including imported goods. Higher incomes increase the ability to purchase imported goods, leading to an expansion of reciprocal demand. Conversely, lower incomes can result in a contraction of reciprocal demand.

Third, tastes and preferences influence reciprocal demand. Differences in consumer preferences between countries can lead to variations in demand for specific goods. If there are a strong preference for certain goods in one country, it can lead to a higher reciprocal demand for those goods.

Lastly, trade policies, such as tariffs or quotas, can impact reciprocal demand. Trade barriers can restrict imports and reduce reciprocal demand for goods subject to those barriers. Conversely, the removal of trade barriers can lead to an expansion of reciprocal demand.

### 3.3.2 Derivation of Offer Curves:

Offer curves are graphical representations of the quantities of goods that a country is willing to export at different world prices, taking into account the relative prices of goods within the country. Offer curves are derived based on the assumptions of perfect competition, constant costs, and fixed resources.

To derive offer curves, we begin with the production possibilities frontier (PPF) of a country. The PPF shows the maximum amount of goods a country can produce given its resources and technology. The slope of the PPF reflects the opportunity cost of producing one good in terms of the other. Assuming a constant opportunity cost, the PPF is a straight line.

Next, we introduce relative prices, which represent the ratio of the price of one good to the price of another. Relative prices influence the allocation of resources between the productions of different goods. If the relative price of good increases, producers have an incentive to allocate more resources to its production, and vice versa.

With the PPF and relative prices, we can derive the offer curve. The offer curve represents the combinations of goods a country is willing to export at different world prices. It is derived by comparing the relative prices in the domestic market with the world prices. When the world price of a good is higher than the domestic relative price, the country has a comparative advantage in producing that good and will export it. Conversely, when the world price is lower than the domestic relative price, the country will import that good.

To illustrate the derivation of offer curves, let's consider a hypothetical example of two countries, Country A and Country B, producing two goods: wheat and cloth. Country A has a comparative advantage in producing wheat, while Country B has a comparative advantage in producing cloth.

Assuming constant opportunity costs, we can draw the PPFs for both countries, showing the maximum amounts of wheat and cloth they can produce given their resources and technology. The slopes of the PPFs represent the opportunity costs of producing one good in terms of the other.

Next, we introduce relative prices in the domestic markets of both countries. These relative prices reflect the ratio of the prices of wheat and cloth within each country. Suppose the relative price of wheat is higher in Country A than in Country B. This implies that the opportunity cost of producing wheat is higher in Country B compared to Country A.

Now, we compare the relative prices in the domestic market with the world prices. If the world price of wheat is higher than the domestic relative price of wheat in Country A, Country A will have an incentive to export wheat. On the other hand, if the world price of cloth is higher than the domestic relative price of cloth in Country B, Country B will have an incentive to export cloth.

By repeating this process for different world prices, we can derive the offer curves for both countries. The offer curves represent the quantities of wheat and cloth that each country is willing to export at different world prices. The offer curve for Country A will have a positive slope for wheat and a negative slope for cloth, while the offer curve for Country B will have a positive slope for cloth and a negative slope for wheat.

### 3.3.3 Insights from Offer Curves :

Offer curves provide several insights into international trade patterns and the effects of relative prices on trade flows. Here are some key insights:

1) **Comparative Advantage:**

   Offer curves demonstrate the concept of comparative advantage. The countries will specialize in producing and exporting the goods in which they have a comparative advantage. The slope of the offer curve reflects the relative opportunity cost of production, and countries will export the goods with a lower opportunity cost.

2) **Terms of Trade:**

   Offer curves highlight the relationship between relative prices and terms of trade. The terms of trade refer to the ratio at which a country can exchange its exports for imports. As the world price of good increases relative to the domestic relative price, a country's terms of trade improve, allowing it to obtain more imports for a given quantity of exports.

3) **Gains from Trade:**

   Offer curves illustrate the gains from trade. When countries engage in trade and specialize according to their comparative advantage, they can consume more of both goods compared to a situation of autarky. The area between the offer curve and the PPF represents the gains from trade, indicating the additional consumption possibilities made possible by trade.

4) **Trade Patterns:**

   Offer curves provide insights into trade patterns and the direction of trade. The relative slopes of the offer curves determine the direction of trade flows. A country with a steeper slope for a particular good has a comparative advantage in producing that good and will export it. By examining the offer curves, we can determine the goods that each country will export or import.

5) **Terms-of-Trade Effects:**
Changes in relative prices and terms of trade can affect the quantities of goods countries are willing to export. If the terms of trade of a country improve, meaning the relative price of its exports increases, it will have an incentive to export more of that good. Similarly, deterioration in terms of trade may lead to a contraction of exports.

## 3.4 Reasons of Unfavourable Terms of Trade:

Normally, underdeveloped countries are exporting primary goods and importing manufactured goods. In this case, terms of trade of underdeveloped countries are not in favour of the country. All underdeveloped countries do not stand on the same level. The following are the main reasons for unfavorable and declining terms of trade of less developed countries:

A) **Prebisch's Arguments:**
Prebisch has given the following arguments explaining the declining tendency of terms of trade of the less developed countries.

1) **Nature of Product:**
The less developed countries are mainly primary producing countries. Their exports mostly include primary products and their imports include capital goods. On the contrary, the developed countries produce and export manufactured goods. The terms of trade between the primary products and manufactured products are generally determined against the former and in favour of the latter.

2) **Effect of Technical Progress:**
Prebisch has argued that industrial countries keep the whole benefit of their technical progress, whereas the primary producing countries transfer a part of the fruits from their own technical progress to the industrial nations.

According to him, money incomes and prices have risen more rapidly than productivity in industrial countries, whereas in the primary producing countries, the gains in productivity have been distributed in the form of price reductions. This has led to the deterioration of terms of trade of the primary producing countries.

3) **Different Market Conditions:**
Export prices in the industrial countries do not fall as a result of technical progress because (a) the manufacturers operate under monopolistic conditions in the product market; and (b) they do not operate under competitive conditions in the factor market, i.e., labour market is dominated by trade unions. Thus, the benefit of the improved technology is not transferred to the consumers in poor countries. The producers in the poor countries, on the other hand operate under competitive

conditions both domestically and internationally. Thus, as a result of technical progress in these countries, prices fall and the benefits flow to the consumers in the rich countries.

**4) Price Movements through Business Cycles:**

Prebisch attributes the contrasting behaviour of prices in the industrial and primary producing countries to the different movements of primary product prices and industrial prices over successive business cycles. The prices of primary products have risen sharply in the prosperous periods and have fallen in the downswing of the business cycle. In contrast, although manufactur-ing prices have risen in the upswing of the cycle, these have not fallen so much in the depression because of the rigidity of industrial wages and price inflexibility due to monopolistic conditions. Thus, over successive cycles, the gap between the prices of the two groups of commodities has widened, and the primary producing countries have suffered an unfavourable movement in their terms of trade.

**5) Disparity in Demand :**

Declining terms of trade of the less developed countries is also due to long-term disparity in the demand for manufactures and primary products.

In the industrial countries, the income elasticity of demand for primary products is inelastic (i.e., less than one), while in the poor countries, the income elasticity of demand for manufactured goods is more elastic (exceeds one).

This is because of two reasons: (a) Due to the operation of Engel's law, as incomes rise, the proportion of expenditure on food declines. Thus, the demand for food increases less rapidly than the rise in income, (b) The demand for raw materials is restricted by competition from synthetic or man-made substitutes.

**B) Other Reasons:**

Some other causes of adverse terms of trade of the less developed countries are as follows:

**1) Backward Technology:**

The less developed countries use backward technology as compared to the developed countries. As a result their relative productivity is low, cost ratios are high, and price structure is also relatively high. This leads to the adverse terms of trade for the poor country, placing it at a disad-vantageous bargaining position.

**2) High Population Growth:**

Most of the less developed countries experience overpopulation and high population growth. As a result, there is high internal demand for the goods and low exportable surplus. Moreover, the import demand of these countries is highly inelastic. This causes their terms of trade to fall.

**3) Lack of Import Substitutes:**

Poor countries are greatly dependant on the advanced countries for their imports and have not developed import substitutes. On the other hand, the advanced countries are not so much dependant on the poor countries because they are capable of producing import substitutes. Thus, the poor countries have weak bargaining position in the international trade.

4) **Lack of Adaptability:**
Unlike, the advanced countries, the less developed countries cannot quickly adapt their supply of goods which are high in demand and whose prices are rising. The reasons for this are: backward technology, market imperfections, immobility of factors of production, etc.

❖❖❖❖❖❖❖❖

## Review Questions

**Q. 1. Answer in 100 Words:**

1) State the Concept of Terms of Trade.
2) Explain the Concept of Static Gains from Trade.
3) State the Concept of Dynamic Gains from Trade.

**Q. 2. Answer in 200 Words:**

1) Discuss in detail about the Gross Barter Terms of Trade.
2) What is Gain from Trade? Explain Kinds of Gains.
3) Write in detail about the Net Barter Terms of Trade.
4) Explain the Importance of Terms of Trade.

**Q. 3. Answer in 400 Words:**

1) What is Terms of Trade? Explain the Importance of Terms of Trade.
2) Discuss in detail about the Types of Terms of Trade.
3) Explain the Determinants of Terms of Trade.
4) State the Reasons of Unfavorable Terms of Trade.
5) Discuss about the Reciprocal Demand and Derivation of Offer Curves.

**Q. 4. Write Short Notes on:**

1) Concept of Terms of Trade.
2) Gain from Trade.
4) Gross Barter Terms of Trade.
5) Net Barter Terms of Trade.
6) Income Terms of Trade.
7) Single Factoral Terms of Trade.
8) Reciprocal Demand.
9) Derivation of Offer Curves.

❖❖❖❖❖❖❖❖

UNIT

# 4

# Balance of Payments



## Introduction:

The Balance of Payment account have significant role in an open economy. An open economy is one which has economic relations with the rest of the world. An economic transaction is an exchange of value, involving a payment or receipts of money in exchange of a good, a service or an asset for which payment is made between the resident of a country with resident of the rest of the world. In 'barter trade', goods are exchanged for goods and in some cases assets are transacted against assets. Some goods are transferred to other as a gift, without expecting payment known in economics as the transfer payments or unilateral transfers. Each of these transactions occurs between the residents of a country and between the economic agents residing in two different countries. If the exchange is happening between the residents of two countries, that transaction in an International economic transaction. An international economic transaction is systematically recorded in the books of accounts of balance of payments. Balance of payments is maintained in a 'Double entry book keeping principle'. Under such principle each transaction is the balance of payments is entered as a Credit or a Debit entry. A 'Credit entry' in Balance of Payments refers to an inflow or that transaction is the one that shows a receipt of funds from the rest of the world.

## 4.1 Balance of Trade:

To arrive at the exact state of international trade position, it is essential to understand the two concepts of Balance of Trade and Balance of Payments. Balance of Payments is a wider term than Balance of Trade because it is the balance of payments which reveals the true picture of international transactions of a country. Balance of Trade refers to the balance of difference between the value of total imports and export of visible material goods.

### 4.1.1 Meaning :

Balance of Trade is the difference between a country's imports and its exports. Balance of trade is the largest component of a country's balance of payments. Debit items include imports, foreign aid, domestic spending abroad and domestic investments abroad. Credit items include exports, foreign spending in the domestic economy and foreign investments in the domestic economy. A country has a trade deficit if it imports more than it exports; the opposite scenario is a trade surplus.

### 4.1.2 Definition :

Following is the definition of balance of trade:

1) **According to Benham :**

   *"Balance of Trade of a country is the relation over a period between the values of her apart and the values of her import."*

### 4.1.3 Types of Balance of Trade :

Balance of trade may be of three types:

1) **Favourable or Surplus Balance of Trade :**

   A country may have favourable or surplus balance of trade when the total value of the goods exported by it is more than the total value of the goods imported by it. (Exports> Imports).

2) **Unfavourable or Deficit Balance of Trade :**

   A country may have unfavourable or deficit balance of trade when the total value of the goods imported by it is more than the total value of the goods exported by it. (Imports > Exports.

3) **Balanced Balance of Trade :**

   A country may have balanced balance of trade when the total value of the goods exported by it is equal to the total value of the goods imported by it. (Exports = Imports)

## 4.2 Balance of Payments:

Balance of payments statistics systematically summarises the economic transactions of an economy with the rest of the World for a specific period. The Reserve Bank of India is responsible for compilation and dissemination of balance of payment data. Balance of payment is broadly consistent with the guidelines contained in the manual of the international monetary fund. The main purpose of the balance of payment is to inform the Government of the international economic position of the nation and to help in formulating it is of monitory, fiscal and trade policies. The Foreign Governments also use the Balance of Payment accounts for the purpose of formulating trade relation with other countries. Other economic agents like bank firms and individual may also depend upon the balance of payment accounts for various purposes. The balance of payment account serves another purpose. The balance of Country's foreign transactions and accompanying issues of the exchange date and reserves has long been a focus of interest for policy members. Thus, the state of balance of payment plays an essential role in providing information to economic agents and Governments.

### 4.2.1 Meaning :

Balance of payment is a summary statement of all economic transactions of the residents of a nation with the residents of rest of the World during a particular period of time. Balance of payment is recorded usually for a calendar year. In other words, balance of payment is a systematic statistical statement or record of the character and dimensions of the country's economic relationship with the rest of the world. Balance of payments is an integral part of national accounts for an open economy.

### 4.2.2 Definitions :

Following are the definitions of balance of payment given by different authors:

1) **Benham:**

   *"Balance of payments of a country is a record of all economic transactions over a period with the rest of the world".*

2) **Kindleberger:**

   *"The balance of payments of a country is systematic record of all economic transactions between its residents and residents of countries."*

3) **James O. Ingram:**

   *"The balance of payments is a summary record of all economic transactions between all residents of one country and the rest of the world during a given period of time."*

4) **P.T. Ellsworth:**

   *"Balance of payment is an annual summary statement of all the transactions between the residents of one country and the rest of the world".*

5) **Walter Krause:**

   *"Balance of payment is a summary of all economic transactions between the residents of country and the residents of the rest of the world during a certain period usually a year."*

### 4.2.3 Importance of Balance of Payment :

From economic point of view, balance of payments for a country is most important. It is evident from the following facts:

1) **Guide to Economic Condition and Direction:**
   Balance of payments is indicative of the economic situation of a country. Countries having always a favourable balance of payments are considered to be economically sound. On the other hand, countries suffering from chronic adverse balance of payments are treated economically sick and unhealthy.
2) **Indicator of Economic Changes:**
   Changes taking place in the economy at different periods of time can best be reflected in its balance of payments position.
3) **Indicator of Foreign Dependency:**
   Balance of payments is an indicator of the extent to which a country is dependent on other countries.
4) **Knowledge of Foreign Receipts and Payments:**
   A country's total receipts and payments are known from its balance of payments.
5) **Knowledge of Capital Foreign Investment:**
   Again, it is balance of payments that tells us about the amount of income earned by the foreigners on their investment in the country. Likewise, the amount of income is earned by the country on its investment abroad.
6) **Indicator of Foreign Trade:**
   Study of balance of payments tells about the state of foreign trade of a country. A country formulates its foreign trade policy on the basis of this knowledge.
7) **Basic of Economic Policy and Planning:**
   Balance of payments makes an important contribution to the formulation of national planning and economic policy. The Government of India is introducing fundamental and structural changes in economic policy due to the state of its balance of payments position.
8) **Helpful for International Financial Organisations:**
   It is on the basis of balance of payments position that international financial institutions determine the amount of financial assistance to be given to a country as IMF has done in case of India.

### 4.2.4 Components of Balance of Payment :

Components of balance of payments are as follows:

1) **Current Account :**
   Current account is a record of exchange of goods and services and unilateral transfers. Readymade garments exported from India or computers imported from the USA are examples of current account transactions. The original entries of

transactions in goods and services, income from foreign investments and unilateral transfers are made in current account.

**i) Balance of Payment on Current Account :**

Balance of payment on current account refers to payments to and by a country for currently purchased or sold goods and services. It also includes interest paid to and by the country on debts as also donations and gifts made to other countries or received from other countries.

**ii) Items in Current Account :**

Items in current account are given below:

**a) Merchandise :**

These are nothing but the imports and exports. Export minus import is termed as trade balance. This difference is also called as net export. Exports are valued at free on board prices. This price includes carriage only from the supplier's premises to the port from which the goods are supposed to be dispatched. Imports are valued at cost, insurance and freight price. This price covers the ex-warehouse price to which the cost of delivery to the docks, dock dues, carriage and insurance as far as the port to which the goods are to be consigned, are to be added. It excludes the cost of delivery from the docks to the purchaser's premises. Trade in merchandise is sometimes called trade invisibles.

**b) Invisibles :**

Trade in invisibles include services, investment and transfer payments. Miscellaneous receipts comprise receipt and payment for professional services, royalties, management fees, subscription fees and so on. Transfer payments include official as well as private transfer payments.

**c) Influences :**

It can be seen that balance of payment on current account influences the level of income of the people in the concerned country directly and almost immediately. Thus, when India imports goods and services from foreign countries and pays for them, that money could have been used to purchase Indian goods and services but it flows out of the country and to that extent reduces the level of income of people in India. On the other hand, when India sells her commodities and services to foreign countries, the producers of those goods and services get income and that pushes up the level of income of people in India. Thus, balance of payments on current account has a direct impact on the level of income of people in a country. Balance of payments on current account is also known as balance of payments on trading account.

**2) Capital Account :**

Capital account is a record of transactions representing foreign assets and liabilities. Examples of capital account transactions include investment in real estate, equities and bonds.

i) **Balance of Payments on Capital Account :**

Balance of payments on capital account refers to payments to and by a country of debts and such other long term claims on each other.

ii) **Items in the Capital Account :**

Items in the capital account are as follows:

a) **Foreign Investment :**

Foreign investment includes the foreign direct investment as well as the investments of the foreign institutional investors, investment in Euro equities and others.

b) **External assistance :**

External assistance in the form of loans, official as well as private, is included in the capital account.

c) **International Monetary Fund :**

International Monetary Fund includes purchases and repurchases from under the various facilities provided by the fund.

iii) **Influences :**

Balance of payments on capital account does not have a direct and immediate impact on the current level of income of the people in a country. It influences the volume of assets which a country holds and that will have effect on the level of income of people in a country in the long run.

## 4.2.5 Difference between Balance of Trade and Balance of Payment :

Difference between Balance of Trade and Balance of Payment explain with following points:

| BASIS OF COMPARISON | BALANCE OF TRADE | BALANCE OF PAYMENT |
|---|---|---|
| **Description** | Balance of trade is a financial statement that captures the nation's import and export of commodities with the rest of the world. | Balance of payment is a financial statement that keeps record value of all the transactions between a countries residence and all the rest of the world during a particular period of time. |
| **Dependability** | Balance of trade is a subset of the balance of payment. | The balance of trade is a major segment of balance of payment. |
| **Record of Physical & Non-physical Items** | Balance of Trade only records the physical items. | Balance of payment records physical items along with non-physical items. |

| | | |
|---|---|---|
| **Capital Receipts** | Balance of Trade does not include capital receipts or payments. | Capital receipts or payments are major parts of the balance of payment. |
| **Calculation** | The balance of trade can be calculated by deducting the value of imports of goods from the value of exports of goods. | Balance of payments can be calculated by adding the balance of payments at the current account and balance of payments at a capital account or by finding out the net balance between inflow of foreign exchange and outflow of foreign exchange. |
| **Unilateral Transfers** | Unilateral transfers are not included in the balance of trade. | Unilateral transfers are major parts of the balance of payments. |
| **Net Effect** | The net effect of balance of trade can be positive, negative or zero. | The net effect of the balance of payments would always be zero. |
| **Entries** | The entries in the balance of trade are related to goods. | Transactions related to goods, services, transfers are included in the balance of payments. |
| **Use** | Balance of trade helps a country to look at the net profit or net loss incurred by the export and import of goods and services. | Balance of payments helps a country in analysis of foreign exchange earnings and transactions. |
| **Importance** | The balance of trade provides half-picture of a country's economic position in comparison to other foreign countries. | Balance of payment provides a complete overview of a country's economic position when compared to other countries. |

## 4.3 Disequilibrium of Balance of Payments:

Disequilibrium in the balance of payments of a country may be either a deficit or a surplus. A deficit or surplus in balance of payments of a country appears when its autonomous receipts do not match its autonomous payments. If autonomous credit receipts exceed autonomous debit payments, there is a surplus in the balance of payments and the disequilibrium is said to be favourable. On the other hand, if autonomous debit payments exceed autonomous credit receipts, there is a deficit in the balance of payments and the disequilibrium is said to be unfavourable or adverse.

### 4.3.1 Causes of Disequilibrium in Balance of Payment:

Various causes of disequilibrium in the balance of payments or adverse balance of payments are as follows:

1) **Development Schemes :**
   The main reason for adverse balance of payments in the developing countries is the huge investment in development schemes in these countries. The propensity to import of the developing countries increases for want of capital for industrialisation. The exports, on the other hand, may not increase because these countries are traditionally primary producing countries. Moreover, the volume of exports may fall because newly created domestic industries may need them. All this leads to structural changes in the balance of payment resulting in structural disequilibrium.
2) **Price-cost Structure :**
   Changes in price-cost structure of export industries affect the volume of exports and create disequilibrium in the balance of payments. Increase in prices due to higher wages, higher cost of raw materials etc. reduce exports and makes the balance of payments unfavourable.
3) **Changes in Foreign Exchange Rates :**
   A change in the rate of exchange is another cause of disequilibrium in the balance of payments. An increase in the external value of money makes imports cheaper and exports dearer; thus, imports increase and exports fall and balance of payments become unfavourable. Similarly, a reduction in the external value of money leads to a reduction in imports and an increase in exports.
4) **Fall in Export Demand :**
   There has been a considerable decline in the export demand for the primary goods of the underdeveloped countries as a result of the large increase in the domestic production of foodstuffs raw materials and substitutes in the rich countries. Similarly, the advanced countries also find a fall in their export demand because of loss of colonial markets. However, the deficit in the balance of payment due to the fall in export demand is more persistent in the underdeveloped countries than in the advanced countries.
5) **Demonstration Effect :**
   The people in the less developed countries tend to follow the consumption patterns of the developed countries. As a result of this demonstration effect, the imports of the less developed countries will increase and create disequilibrium in the balance of payments.

**6) International Borrowing and Lending :**

International borrowing and lending is another reason for the disequilibrium in the balance of payments. The borrowing country tends to have unfavourable balance of payments while the lending country tends to have favourable balance of payments.

**7) Cyclical Fluctuations :**

Cyclical fluctuations cause cyclical disequilibrium in the balance of payments. During depression, the incomes of the people in foreign countries fall. As a result, the exports of these countries tend to decline which, in turn, produces disequilibrium in the home country's balance of payment.

**8) Newly Independent Countries :**

The newly independent countries, in order to develop international relations, incur huge amounts of expenditure on the establishment of embassies, missions etc. in other countries. This adversely affects the balance of payments position.

**9) Population Explosion :**

Another important reason for adverse balance of payments in the poor countries is population explosion. Rapid growth of population in countries like India increases imports and decreases the capacity to export.

**10) Natural Factors :**

Natural calamities such as droughts, floods etc. adversely affect the production in the country. As a result, the exports fall, the imports increase and the country experiences deficit in its balance of payments.

## 4.3.2 Consequences of Disequilibrium in Balance of Payment:

Disequilibrium in the Balance of Payments refers to a situation where the total inflows and outflows of foreign exchange in an economy are not balanced over a specific period. It occurs when a country is experiencing either a persistent surplus or deficit in its external transactions. Disequilibrium in the Balance of Payments can have various consequences for an economy, which can range from short-term adjustments to long-term structural imbalances. In following discussion, we will discuss the consequences of disequilibrium in the Balance of Payments.

**1) Exchange Rate Pressure:**

A persistent deficit in the Balance of Payments puts downward pressure on a country's currency. To finance the deficit, the country needs to sell more of its currency to buy foreign currency, increasing the supply of its currency in the foreign exchange market. This excess supply of currency leads to depreciation, which can erode the purchasing power of the domestic currency. A depreciated currency makes imports more expensive, contributing to inflationary pressures.

**2) Current Account Adjustment:**

Disequilibrium in the Balance of Payments is typically reflected in the current account. A persistent deficit implies that a country is importing more goods and services than it is exporting. This can lead to a loss of competitiveness in domestic industries, as they face competition from cheaper imports. To correct the imbalance, countries may need to adjust their production and consumption patterns, such as increasing exports, reducing imports, or improving productivity in import-competing industries. These adjustments can involve short-term costs and challenges, including layoffs, sectoral shifts, and changes in consumption patterns.

3) **Accumulation of External Debt:**

A sustained deficit in the Balance of Payments requires financing from external sources, leading to an accumulation of external debt. Countries with persistent deficits rely on borrowing to finance the gap between imports and exports. As the debt accumulates, the country becomes increasingly vulnerable to external shocks and changes in global financing conditions. High levels of external debt can lead to increased debt service burdens, higher interest payments, and potential risks of default, which can have severe implications for an economy's stability and creditworthiness.

4) **Loss of Reserves and Financial Vulnerability:**

A persistent deficit in the Balance of Payments can deplete a country's foreign exchange reserves. To finance the deficit, countries may draw down their reserves, which serve as a buffer to manage external shocks and maintain stability. Depletion of reserves can leave the country vulnerable to sudden capital outflows or external crises. In extreme cases, a loss of reserves can lead to a currency crisis, with severe depreciation, capital flight, and financial instability.

5) **Macroeconomic Imbalances:**

Disequilibrium in the Balance of Payments can create broader macroeconomic imbalances within an economy. A persistent deficit can contribute to inflationary pressures, as the depreciation of the currency raises the cost of imported goods. It can also lead to reduced investment and slower economic growth if the deficit is not addressed effectively. On the other hand, a persistent surplus can create challenges as well, such as an overvalued currency, reduced competitiveness in export sectors, and potential overheating in the domestic economy.

6) **Policy Challenges:**

Disequilibrium in the Balance of Payments poses significant policy challenges for policymakers. Addressing the imbalance requires implementing appropriate policy measures to promote a sustainable external position. This can involve a combination of fiscal policy, monetary policy, exchange rate policy, and structural reforms. However, policy adjustments can be politically challenging and may face resistance from different stakeholders, making it difficult to achieve consensus and implement necessary reforms.

**7) Impact on Investment and Economic Growth:**

Disequilibrium in the Balance of Payments can affect investment and economic growth. A persistent deficit may signal a lack of competitiveness in the economy, deterring foreign direct investment (FDI) and reducing domestic investment. It can also limit the availability of foreign capital inflows, which are essential for financing investment projects. Moreover, a large external imbalance can undermine investor confidence, leading to capital flight and a slowdown in economic growth.

**8) Trade Protectionism:**

Prolonged disequilibrium in the Balance of Payments can trigger protectionist sentiments and trade barriers. Countries with persistent deficits may resort to measures such as tariffs, quotas, or subsidies to protect domestic industries and reduce imports. These protectionist measures can harm international trade relationships, lead to retaliatory actions from trading partners, and distort global trade patterns. Such trade conflicts can further exacerbate the imbalances and hinder economic growth.

## 4.4 Measures to Correct Disequilibrium in the Balance of Payments:

Persistent disequilibrium in the balance of payments particularly a deficit in balance of payments is undesirable because it (a) weakens the country's economic position at the international level and (b) affects the progress of the economy adversely. It must be cured by taking appropriate measures. There are many measures to correct disequilibrium in the balance of payments. Important among them are discussed below:

**1) Deflation :**

In the wake of deficit in a nation's balance of payments, it can resort to tight monetary policy. The currency authority may try to lower the prices by reducing the quantity of money in circulation or follow a deflationary monetary policy. Deflation is the classical medicine for correcting the deficit in the balance of payments. Deflation refers to the policy of reducing the quantity of money in order to reduce the prices and the money income of the people. This is done by the central bank of the country through raising the bank rate by selling the securities in the open market and by other methods can reduce the volume of credit in the economy which will lead to a fall in prices and money income of the people. Fall in prices will stimulate exports and reduction in income checks imports. Thus, deflationary policy restores equilibrium to the balance:

**a)** By encouraging exports through reduction in their prices and

**b)** By discouraging imports through the reduction in incomes at home.

Moreover, a higher interest rate in the domestic market will attract foreign funds which can be used for correcting disequilibrium. However, deflation is not considered a suitable method to correct adverse balance of payments because of the following reasons:

a) Deflation means reduction in income or wages which is strongly opposed by the trade unions.

b) Deflation causes unemployment and suffering to the working class.

c) In a developing economy, expansionary monetary policy rather than contractionary (deflationary) monetary policy is required to meet the developmental needs.

2) **Depreciation :**

Another method of correcting disequilibrium in the balance of payments is depreciation or appreciation of the exchange rate. Deprecation means a fall in the rate of exchange of one currency (home currency) in terms of another (foreign currency). A currency will depreciate when its supply in the foreign exchange market is large in relation to its demand. In other words, a currency is said to depreciate if its value falls in terms of foreign currencies, i.e., if more domestic currency is required to buy a unit of foreign currency. An appreciation on the other hand is the rise in the value of a currency relative to the foreign currency. Depreciation helps a country to achieve a favourable balance of payments by checking imports and stimulating exports. The following are the defects of this method:

a) It is not suitable for a country which follows a fixed exchange rate system.

b) It makes international trade risky and, thus, reduces the volume of trade.

c) The terms of trade go against the country whose currency depreciates because the foreign goods have become costlier than the local goods and the country has to export more to pay for the same volume of imports.

d) Experience of certain countries has indicated that exchange depreciation may generate inflationary pressure by increasing the domestic price level and money income.

e) The success of the method of exchange depreciation depends upon the cooperation of other countries. If other countries also start depreciating their exchange rates then these methods will not benefit any country.

3) **Devaluation :**

Devaluation refers to the official reduction of the external values of a currency. The difference between devaluation and depreciation is that while devaluation means the lowering of external value of a currency by the government, depreciation means an automatic fall in the external value of the currency by the market forces; the former is arbitrary and the latter is the result of market mechanism. Thus, devaluation serves only as an alternative method to depreciation. Both the methods imply the same thing, i.e., decrease in the value of a currency in terms of foreign currencies. Both the methods can be used to produce the same effects; they discourage imports, encourage exports and, thus, lead to a reduction in the balance of payments deficit.

The success of the method of devaluation depends upon the following conditions:

a) The elasticity of demand for the country's exports should be greater than unity.

b) The elasticity of demand for the country's imports should be greater than unity.

c) The exports of the country should be non-traditional and the increasingly demanded from other countries.

d) The domestic price should not rise and should remain stable after devaluation.

e) Other countries should not retaliate by resorting to corresponding devaluation. Such a retaliatory measure will offset each other's gain.

4) **Exchange Control :**

Exchange control is the most widely used method for correcting disequilibrium in the balance of payments. Exchange control refers to the control over the use of foreign exchange by the central bank. Under this method, all the exporters are directed by the central bank to surrender their foreign exchange earnings. Foreign exchange is rationed among the licenced importers. Only essential imports are permitted. Exchange control is the most direct method of restricting a country's import. The major drawback of this method is that it deals with the deficit only and not its causes. Rather it may aggravate these causes and, thus, may create a more basic disequilibrium. In short, exchange control does not provide a permanent solution for a chronic disequilibrium.

5) **Tariffs :**

Tariffs are duties (taxes) imposed on imports. When tariffs are imposed, the prices of imports would increase to the extent of tariff. The increased prices will reduce the demand for imported goods and at the same time, induce domestic producers to produce more of import substitutes. Non-essential imports can be drastically reduced by imposing a very high rate of tariff.

6) **Quotas :**

Under the quota system, the government may fix and permit the maximum quantity or value of a commodity to be imported during a given period. By restricting imports through the quota system, the deficit is reduced and the balance of payments position is improved.

7) **Fiscal Policy Adjustments:**

Governments can use fiscal policy to address imbalances in the Balance of Payments. In the case of a deficit, fiscal measures can include reducing government spending or increasing taxes to reduce domestic demand and imports. Conversely, if there is a surplus, governments can stimulate domestic demand through increased government spending or tax cuts to encourage imports.

8) **Monetary Policy Interventions:**

Central banks can utilize monetary policy tools to address imbalances in the Balance of Payments. For a deficit, the central bank can tighten monetary policy by increasing interest rates to reduce domestic demand and discourage imports.

Conversely, if there is a surplus, the central bank can adopt an expansionary monetary policy by reducing interest rates to stimulate domestic demand and encourage imports.

9) **Exchange Rate Adjustments:**

Adjusting the exchange rate can be an effective measure to correct imbalances. If a country has a deficit, a depreciation of the domestic currency can make exports cheaper and imports relatively more expensive, thus promoting exports and reducing imports. Conversely, if there is a surplus, an appreciation of the domestic currency can make imports cheaper and exports relatively more expensive, thereby discouraging imports and promoting exports.

10) **Structural Reforms:**

Structural reforms are long-term measures aimed at improving the competitiveness and productivity of the economy. These reforms can include deregulation, trade liberalization, investment in infrastructure, labor market reforms, and improvements in the business environment. By enhancing the efficiency and competitiveness of domestic industries, structural reforms can help correct imbalances in the Balance of Payments.

11) **Trade Policy Adjustments:**

Countries can consider trade policy adjustments to address imbalances. For instance, if a country has a deficit, it can focus on promoting export-oriented industries by providing incentives, reducing export barriers, or negotiating trade agreements that facilitate market access for its products. On the other hand, if there is a surplus, measures can be taken to promote import substitution industries, safeguard domestic industries, or negotiate trade agreements that protect sensitive sectors.

12) **Promotion of Investment and Export Diversification:**

Governments can implement policies to attract foreign direct investment (FDI) and promote export diversification. This can involve providing incentives for investment, improving the investment climate, enhancing infrastructure, developing export-oriented industries, and supporting research and development activities. By diversifying exports and attracting investment, countries can reduce reliance on specific sectors and markets, reducing vulnerability to imbalances.

13) **Strengthening Domestic Savings:**

Countries with deficits often rely on foreign borrowing to finance the gap between imports and exports. To address this, efforts can be made to increase domestic savings and reduce reliance on external financing. Encouraging household savings, improving financial literacy, and implementing policies that promote investment in productive sectors can help boost domestic savings.

**14) Addressing Structural Issues:**

Disequilibrium in the Balance of Payments can be caused by underlying structural issues such as a lack of competitiveness, inefficient production processes, or inadequate infrastructure. Addressing these structural issues through targeted policies and investments can help improve productivity, reduce costs, and enhance the overall competitiveness of the economy.

❖❖❖❖❖❖❖❖❖

## Review Questions

**Q. 2. Answer in 100 Words:**

1) State the Concept of Balance of Trade.
2) Explain the Concept of Balance of Payments.
3) State the Importance of Balance of Payments.

**Q. 3. Answer in 200 Words:**

1) State the Difference between Balance of Trade and Balance of Payments.
2) What is Balance of Trade? Explain the Types of Balance of Trade.
3) Explain the Consequences of Disequilibrium in Balance of Payments.

**Q. 4. Answer in 400 Words:**

1) What is Balance of Payments? Explain the Components of Balance of Payments.
2) Explain the Causes of Disequilibrium in Balance of Payments.
3) Discuss the Measures to Correct Disequilibrium in Balance of Payment.

**Q. 1. Answer in 20 Words:**

1) Balance of Trade.
2) Balance of Payments.
4) Components of Balance of Payments.
6) Causes of Disequilibrium in Balance of Payment.
7) Measures to correct Disequilibrium in Balance of Payment.

❖❖❖❖❖❖❖❖❖